SIMPLE AND CREATIVE IDEAS
FOR MAKING LIFELONG MEMORIES

5 2

UNCOMMON FAMILY ADVENTURES

SIMPLE AND CREATIVE IDEAS
FOR MAKING LIFELONG MEMORIES

52

UNCOMMON FAMILY ADVENTURES

RANDY SOUTHERN

MOODY PUBLISHERS
CHICAGO

Unless otherwise noted, Scripture quotations are taken from the Holy Bible, New
International Version®, NIV®. Copyright © 1973, 1978, 1984, 2011 by Biblica, Inc.™
Used by permission of Zondervan. All rights reserved worldwide. www.zondervan.com.
The "NIV" and "New International Version" are trademarks registered in the United
States Patent and Trademark Office by Biblica, Inc.™

Scripture quotations marked ESV are taken from The ESV® Bible (The Holy Bible,
English Standard Version®), copyright © 2001 by Crossway, a publishing ministry
of Good News Publishers. Used by permission. All rights reserved.

Edited by Connor Sterchi and Peter Blankenship
Interior and cover design: Julia Ryan / DesignByJulia.com
Cover images: puppy: © Shutterstock/Neil Lockhart; abstract-pattern: © Shutterstock/
balabolka; "2": © Shutterstock/Roman Siggev; figure illustrations: Julia Ryan
Interior images: all chapter spot-illustrations: © Shutterstock/Ron and Joe; ; abstract-pattern
© Shutterstock/Neil Lockhart; time/cost/locale icons: Julia Ryan / DesignByJulia.com

Library of Congress Cataloging-in-Publication Data

Names: Southern, Randy, author.
Title: 52 uncommon family adventures / Randy Southern.
Description: Chicago : Moody Publishers, [2019] | Includes index. |
   Identifiers: LCCN 2019017451 (print) | LCCN 2019019968 (ebook) | ISBN
   9780802497987 | ISBN 9780802419392
Subjects: LCSH: Families--Religious life. | Family recreation.
Classification: LCC BV4526.3 (ebook) | LCC BV4526.3 .S68 2019 (print) | DDC
   249--dc23
LC record available at https://lccn.loc.gov/2019017451

We hope you enjoy this book from Moody Publishers. Our goal is to provide high-quality,
thought-provoking books and products that connect truth to your real needs and
challenges. For more information on other books and products written and produced
from a biblical perspective, go to www.moodypublishers.com or write to:

Moody Publishers
820 N. LaSalle Boulevard
Chicago, IL 60610

1 3 5 7 9 10 8 6 4 2

Printed in the United States of America

CONTENTS

INTRODUCTION BY GARY CHAPMAN, PAGE 7

INTRODUCTION
BY GARY CHAPMAN

Creating adventure in the family keeps life from becoming routine. We are all creatures of habit. We tend to do the same things in the same way, at the same time every day. There is value in being organized, but sometimes we need to break out of the routine and do something a little bit crazy. It is adventure that keeps family life exciting.

Children love adventure, but often parents have to plan it and supervise it. *52 Uncommon Family Adventures* is a practical resource for parents. It also has the advantage of relating the five love languages to the various adventures. What could be better than having fun and expressing love to your children at the same time?

I think most parents want their children to grow up with pleasant childhood memories. However, it takes time and a bit of creativity to build such memories. Some of us are more creative than others, but almost all of us could use a little help in coming up with ideas that will be meaningful and fun. Randy Southern gives not only ideas, but explains how to plan for and implement family adventures.

One of the things I think most parents will appreciate is his suggested devotional ideas that accompany each of the adventures. Reading the Scriptures and discussing them in a fun setting gives the children an appreciation for the Bible. It also provides parents with an opportunity to relate the Bible to daily life experiences.

As the coauthor of *The 5 Love Languages of Children*, I am always encouraged to see unique ways to help parents keep the love languages on the front burner. When parents discover the love language of each child and speak that language often, the child feels loved. When the children understand that their sister has a love language, their brother has a love language, their mom and their dad have a love language, they are learning an insight that will serve them well throughout life. As they practice speaking each other's love language, the children are developing a skill that will help them be better parents in years to come.

You may not find time to plan a "family adventure" each week, but that is not the objective. One of the characteristics of an adventure is that it is not always scheduled. So, surprise the children by saying, "Tomorrow night we are going to have an adventure." As they have fun, they will come to anticipate your announcements of "adventure night."

Of course you will want to pick from *52 Uncommon Family Adventures* those that relate best to your children's age and stage of development. Some you will find work well with a six-year-old, but not so well with a three-year-old. However, all children love adventure, even grown children who are now parents. So, make the most of this helpful resource as a means of creating memories for your children and for their parents!

WHAT ARE THE FIVE LOVE LANGUAGES?
WHAT IS YOURS?

WORDS OF AFFIRMATION: Actions don't always speak louder than words. If this is your love language, unsolicited compliments mean the world to you. Hearing the words "I love you" is important—hearing the reasons behind that love sends your spirits skyward.

QUALITY TIME: Nothing says "I love you" like full, undivided attention. Being there for a person whose love language is Quality Time is critical, but really being there—with the TV off, fork and knife down, and all chores and tasks on standby— makes him or her feel truly special and loved.

RECEIVING GIFTS: The receiver of gifts thrives on the love, thoughtfulness, and effort behind the gift. If you speak this language, the perfect gift or gesture shows that you are known, you are cared for, and you are prized above whatever was sacrificed to bring the gift to you.

ACTS OF SERVICE: Anything you do to ease the burden of responsibilities weighing on an Acts of Service person will speak volumes. The words he or she most wants to hear: "Let me do that for you."

PHYSICAL TOUCH: A person whose primary language is Physical Touch enjoys hugs, pats on the back, and thoughtful touches on the arm. These can all be ways to show excitement, concern, care, and love.

Visit 5lovelanguages.com to discover your primary love language!

KEY

TIME COMMITMENT

ONE HOUR　　HALF DAY　　FULL DAY

COST

FREE　　LOW COST　　MODERATE COST

LOCALE

INDOORS　　OUTDOORS

LOVE LANGUAGE

WORDS OF AFFIRMATION　　ACTS OF SERVICE　　RECEIVING GIFTS　　QUALITY TIME　　PHYSICAL TOUCH

THANK-YOU CARDS

Single out the people who have made a difference in your lives with heartfelt notes of gratitude.

1

GETTING READY

One of the best ways to encourage the habit of writing thank-you cards is to buy your kids personalized stationery. You can order cards and envelopes with your kids' names embossed on them, in their favorite colors, or with a background or logo that features something they like.

ADVENTURE TIME

Encourage each of your family members to think of someone in his or her life who deserves a thank you—not necessarily for a specific gift or act of kindness, but for always being a positive presence. Spend some time as a family writing cards to the people you choose.

Encourage your family members to write about specific things their person has done and what it meant to them. For example, if the person made it a point to attend recitals and games, your family member might talk about what it meant to see him or her in the crowd. If your family members have trouble thinking of specific things to write about, brainstorm some ideas as a family that they can use.

THAT REMINDS ME

List some of the different ways to say thank you in foreign languages. In Spanish, it's "Gracias." In French, it's "Merci." In Italian, it's "Grazie." In Japanese, it's "Arigato" (ありがとう). In German, it's "Danke sehr." In Chinese, it's "do jeh" (多謝).

Talk about other ways people say thank you. In American Sign Language, you put the fingers of your open hand to your mouth, with your palm facing inward, and then extend them away from your mouth. In the theater, actors take a bow. In sports, athletes tap their chests. Some people simply offer a slight head nod.

Talk about the difference between offering a polite thank you and expressing heartfelt gratitude. A person with good manners may say thank you dozens of times a day. It's a nice thing to do, but it's not necessarily meaningful. A heartfelt expression of gratitude, on the other hand, can make a difference in a person's life. Sometimes kind people need to hear about the impact their kindness has had.

FAMILY DEVOTIONS

Have someone read Philippians 1:3–5 ("I thank my God every time I remember you. In all my prayers for all of you, I always pray with joy because of your partnership in the gospel from the first day until now"). Explain that the apostle Paul used these words to greet the church in Philippi, which had faithfully supported his ministry.

Ask, *How does this passage apply to the person you wrote your thank-you card to?* Share your own thoughts first. Talk a little about the person to whom you're writing your thank-you card. What is it that you thank God for when you think of that person? What is it about the person that brings you joy?

Ask, *How can you become this type of person in someone else's life?* If no one else mentions it, suggest that it requires an investment of yourself. You do it by giving your time, attention, and resources in order to make the person's life better.

LANGUAGE OF THE DAY

This adventure is practically custom-made for someone whose primary love language is Words of Affirmation. If one of your family members fits that bill, write that person a heartfelt thank-you note for the things they do around the house, for the joy they bring to your life, and for anything else you can think of. The more specific you are in your gratitude and praise, the more weight your words will carry.

TO NEXT ADVENTURE

ALL THINGS NERF

2

Have some fun with the softest toys in your house.

GETTING READY

All you need for this quick adventure is a variety of Nerf® products and safety goggles for everyone. If your own Nerf collection isn't enough to sustain an hour-long adventure, see if you can borrow some from your friends and neighbors.

ADVENTURE TIME

Depending on what you have in your Nerf collection, there are any number of games and challenges you can do.

If you have a Nerf hoop and ball, play a game of "Pig" or "Horse." Make sure you incorporate your surroundings by bouncing shots off the walls, ceiling, and furniture.

If you have a Nerf football, set up a throwing-skills challenge. At one station, a contestant may have to knock over a stack of aluminum cans. At another station, he or she may have to throw the ball through a tire swing or hula hoop.

If you have two small Nerf guns, holsters, and ammo (plus two safety goggles), try reenacting pistol duels or gunfights from the Old West. Duelists may face each other, draw and fire when someone says, "Go," or they may stand back to back, take five steps and then turn and fire.

If you have a large arsenal of Nerf weapons, you may want to set up a battle zone in your basement or backyard and declare an all-out Nerf family war.

If you prefer a less confrontational use of your Nerf guns, set up a shooting range, using a variety of creative targets. For example, you might set up a domino chain on a table and then see who can shoot the first domino to trigger the chain reaction.

 ## THAT REMINDS ME

Say something like this: *One of the reasons Nerf stuff is so fun to play with is that it doesn't hurt when it hits you. Some people say the same is true for words. They quote the old saying, "Sticks and stones may break my bones, but words will never harm me." Do you believe that's true?* You may want to break the ice here with an example from your own life when words *did* hurt you. Encourage the rest of your family members to share similar experiences.

Talk about how you reacted to the harmful words. Did you try to hurt the person who hurt you? Did you confront the person and tell him or her how you felt? Did you tell someone else, perhaps a teacher or parent? Did you get emotional in front of the person? Or did you just ignore it and pretend that it didn't bother you? If you had it to do over again, how would you react? Encourage your family members to talk about their reactions as well. If they had it to do over again, would they react differently?

Talk about the lasting effects the person's words had on you. If no one else mentions it, point out that harmful words are a form of bullying, especially if they continue over time. And bullying can cause people to become fearful or depressed or to lose confidence in themselves.

FAMILY DEVOTIONS

Have someone read 2 Timothy 1:7 ("For the Spirit God gave us does not make us timid, but gives us power, love and self-discipline"). Explain that when a person accepts Christ as

Savior, God's Holy Spirit enters that person's life and changes it forever. Ask, *What causes people to be timid?* If no one else mentions

it, suggest that fear and a lack of confidence can cause someone to be timid—emotions that are brought on by negative experiences with others.

Have someone read Deuteronomy 31:6 ("Be strong and courageous. Do not be afraid or terrified because of them, for the LORD your God goes with you; he will never leave you nor forsake you"). Ask, *How does God's presence keep us from being scared—or negatively affected by others?* Encourage each of your family members to offer a response.

LANGUAGE OF THE DAY

If Receiving Gifts is the primary love language of a Nerf-loving member of your family, present him or her with a small Nerf gun or a Nerf basketball hoop as a memento of this adventure.

TO NEXT ADVENTURE

HIDE-AND-SEEK

3

This perennial kids' favorite can be turned into an adventure for all ages with just a few tweaks.

GETTING READY

How do you prepare for a game of hide-and-seek? You scout ideal locations for the game ahead of time. Your goal is to find an area that's relatively confined so that the seeking doesn't take forever. On the other hand, you want a place that offers plenty of hiding places for people big and small. The perimeter of an empty school building could work, as could a neighborhood park or a small forest preserve.

ADVENTURE TIME

You probably don't need a lot of instructions on how to play hide-and-seek. One player ("It") gives everyone else time to hide and then tries to find them. After everyone is found, another player becomes "It" and everyone else hides again.

What you might want to consider, especially if your kids are older, are variations on the game to make it more challenging, fun, or interesting. For example, you might play immediately after a snowfall. Your family members will have to figure out how to hide without leaving tracks in the snow.

Another option is to play in the dark. Let the person who is "It" use a high-beam flashlight when he or she is seeking.

You can also switch things up and play a few rounds in which

▶ one person hides and everyone else seeks. This variation is called Sardines. (Hopefully the first hider does not hide somewhere too cramped.)

▶ everyone tries to find the *worst* possible hiding place.

▶ everyone must hide within twenty yards of one another.

▶ once the seeker finds a hider, that hider accompanies the seeker in their search for people. If the hider spots another hider before the seeker does, the caught hider and hider wave at each other, which releases the caught hider and allows them to hide again. This version puts a lot of pressure on the seeker.

If you have a young player who has difficulty seeking, add a "Marco Polo" twist to the game. Every time the young seeker shouts "Marco!" the other players must call out "Polo!" from their hiding places.

THAT REMINDS ME

One of the harrowing rites of parenthood is trying to find a lost child. If you have a story about losing track of one of your children, tell it. Talk about the impact it had on you—the panic you felt, the guilt you experienced, or perhaps the nightmares you had afterward. Relive the joy and relief you felt when you found your child. It would be interesting to get your child's perspective on the incident, if he or she remembers it.

Point out that the world is a big place. Sometimes people feel like they're lost and don't know where to go or what to do. Assure your family members that if they ever find themselves in that situation, they always have three places to turn. The first is God, and the other two are your church and your family. Emphasize the importance of supporting and encouraging one another.

FAMILY DEVOTIONS

Summarize the story of Adam and Eve's temptation in the garden of Eden: how God gave them permission to eat from any tree in the garden except one, how the serpent tempted them to eat the forbidden fruit, and how Adam and Eve gave in to the temptation and sinned.

Ask, *When God came to visit them in the garden after they had sinned, what did Adam and Eve do?* Have someone read the answer in Genesis 3:8 ("they hid from the LORD God among the trees of the garden"). Help your kids understand that Adam and Eve hid from God because they were ashamed.

Say something like this: *King David, who lived many, many, many centuries after Adam and Eve, did some bad things, too. And he thought about hiding from God as well. But then he realized something very important.*

Read together Psalm 139:1–12. Help your kids understand that no one can hide from God because He sees everything. What's more, because He created us, He knows everything about us. He knows us better than we know ourselves.

And He loves us—even when we do wrong. It hurts Him, but He still loves us.

Read together the Parable of the Lost Sheep in Luke 15:1–7. Ask, *How does it make you feel to know that God will never give up on you?*

Pray together, praising God for His love and concern for us. Ask His forgiveness for the times when you "go astray." Ask Him to guide your family in making decisions that honor Him.

 ## LANGUAGE OF THE DAY

You can make this adventure especially meaningful for someone whose primary love language is Words of Affirmation. When it's your turn to seek, narrate your search by calling out your kids (and spouse) by their accomplishments.

For example, you might say, "I'm looking for the talented young man who played the beautiful French horn solo at the Christmas concert" or "I'm looking for the unstoppable young woman who scored two goals in a playoff game last season."

INTERVIEWS

4 Get to know your family members better by conducting one-on-one interviews.

GETTING READY

All you *really* need for this activity is a list of interesting questions. Beyond that, you can add some production value to your interview by creating a "set"—two chairs in front of an interesting backdrop, plus a coffee table and a couple of mugs filled with your favorite beverages.

If you choose to personalize the activity to fit someone's primary love language (see "Language of the Day"), you'll need to record and edit questions from other people and have them ready to play back during your interview.

ADVENTURE TIME

You can learn a lot about people by asking the right questions, even if you've lived with them for most of your life. That's the idea behind this quick adventure. Interview your family members—and let them interview you—using carefully chosen questions. Make sure that everyone has a turn in the "hot seat." To keep things interesting and fast-moving, you may want to set a five-minute time limit for each interview. Encourage family members to offer thoughtful answers, instead of trying to be funny. (In fact, you might want to set the tone by agreeing to be interviewed first.) Record the interviews for posterity. You may want to have your family members switch roles—interviewer, interviewee, cameraperson, audience member—after each interview.

Depending on the person in the hot seat, you might ask such questions as

- ▶ What were you afraid of when you were younger? How did you overcome your fear?

- ▶ When were you most proud of yourself?

- ▶ If you could talk to anyone—living or dead—for one hour, who would you choose and why? What would you talk about?

- ▶ Where do you see yourself in ten years? Where would you like to live? What would you like to be doing?

- ▶ If you could do one thing over again, what would it be?

THAT REMINDS ME

Talk about a time when you discovered something surprising about a friend or family member, just by asking a simple question or showing an interest in what the person had to say. Point out that you can learn a lot about other people by asking the right questions and listening to their responses. You can also show yourself to be a valuable friend in the process. Most people like to share their thoughts, especially if they know someone is listening.

Spend a few minutes talking about the kind of questions that draw people out—questions that require more than a one-word answer but that don't seem too nosy or invasive.

FAMILY DEVOTIONS

Say something like this: *It's only natural that we should be curious about one another—and about everyone we meet. Each of us is a masterpiece of God's creativity.*

Have someone read Psalm 139:14 ("I praise you because I am fearfully and wonderfully made; your works are wonderful, I know that full well"). Recall some of the specific things you learned about one another during your interviews.

Say something like this: *Our interests, skills, abilities and quirks—the things that make us unique—all come from God. He put them inside us for a reason. So the more we learn about one another, the more we learn about Him.*

Pray together, thanking God for making each person in your family a unique creation. Thank Him for the opportunity to get to know—and be known by—others. Ask Him to give you wisdom when it comes to recognizing and appreciating people's uniqueness—as well as in asking the right questions and listening in a way that draws people out. Ask Him to surround your family with people who are equally appreciative of and curious about your unique personalities.

LANGUAGE OF THE DAY

This adventure can be especially meaningful for someone whose primary love language is Words of Affirmation. Recruit a few friends, extended family members, mentors, teachers, and others to record a few flattering questions for the person you want to honor. Depending on their connection to your family member, they might ask anything from "What's your secret for shooting free throws so well?" to "How did you learn to make people laugh?" Give your interviewee a chance to bask in the limelight as he or she answers the questions.

TO NEXT ADVENTURE

SOMETHING OLD

5

Create some new memories by re-creating
a favorite old photograph.

GETTING READY

If you're doing this on the spur-of-the-moment, the
only preparation you need is to find an old photo to
re-create. If you want to put some extra effort into
it, you can try to match the details in the photo
as accurately as possible. That may involve finding
clothes that match those in the original photo—and
perhaps styling your family's hair to match the hairstyles in the photo. If possible, you may also want
to revisit the location where the original photo was
taken or find a place that looks very much like it.

ADVENTURE TIME

The key to success with this adventure is finding
the right photograph to re-create. The ideal photo

will feature all of your children. The goofier and more childlike their poses are, the more fun they will be to re-create. If possible, have an enlarged version of the original photo on hand so that your family members can refer to it as they pose.

You'll also need to consider the camera height and angle used in the original photo. The more closely you can approximate them, the more effective your re-creation will be. Spend as much time as your family will tolerate getting the poses right. Matching the facial expressions in the original is also important. That's why it's vital to have someone—ideally someone who's not in the picture—serve as a director for the shoot. The director can look at the original and stage the re-creation accordingly, making sure that one person's head is tilted just right, that one person's cheesy grin is showing enough teeth, and that another person's hand is positioned just right on someone else's shoulder. Keep shooting until you get the re-creation you're looking for.

If you're satisfied with the results, post the two photos side by side on your social media account for all to enjoy.

THAT REMINDS ME

Spend some time reminiscing about what was going on in your family when the original photograph was taken. If your kids were in school, talk about what grades they were in, who their teachers were, who their friends were, what sports or activities they were involved in, what books, movies, songs, or celebrities they were obsessed with—anything you can remember.

But don't get lost in nostalgia. Spend an equal amount of time talking about what's going on in your family now. Share your excitement about what your kids are doing. Point out that a few years from now, you'll be looking back with nostalgia at the things that are happening right now.

FAMILY DEVOTIONS

Explain that there's a family in the Bible who would have had a hard time re-creating an old photo—if photography had existed back then. Summarize the story of Joseph in Genesis 37–50:

- ▶ Joseph's ten older brothers hated him so much that they sold him as a slave.

- ▶ He ended up in Egypt, where he was thrown in prison for something he didn't do.

- ▶ Eventually he became a powerful man in Egypt.

- ▶ When a famine hit the land, Joseph was in charge of distributing food.

- ▶ His brothers, whom he hadn't seen since they betrayed him, came to Egypt for food. Joseph recognized them, but they didn't recognize him.

- ▶ When he finally revealed his identity, they were terrified.

Say something like this: *Joseph's brothers ruined Joseph's life and tore their family apart. How could they ever hope to be reunited?*

Have someone read Genesis 50:19–20 ("But Joseph said to them, 'Don't be afraid. Am I in the place of God? You intended to harm me, but God intended it for good to accomplish what is now being done, the saving of many lives'").

Say something like this: *Joseph was able to forgive his brothers and reunite his family because he could see the big picture. He knew that no matter how bad things seemed, God would bring something good from it. His brothers' betrayal ultimately put Joseph in a position to save his family. And if God can work through that kind of family dysfunction, He can work through anything.*

Pray together, thanking God for the love that binds your family. Ask Him to continue to bring good from situations that seem anything but good.

LANGUAGE OF THE DAY

This adventure can serve as a nice pick-me-up for someone whose primary love language is Quality Time. Choose a photograph in which that family member is the center of attention. Celebrate that person as you re-create the photo. Encourage everyone to share special memories of him or her.

TO NEXT ADVENTURE

PILLOW FIGHT

6

Blow off some steam and laugh yourselves silly as you wallop one another in the softest way possible.

GETTING READY

The best way to prepare for a pillow fight is to create a safe place for it to happen. Remove furniture with hard surfaces or sharp edges, as well as lamps and any other breakables. Depending on your preferred level of safety, cover the floor with mattresses, comforters, blankets, and cushions. Check the pillows for zippers or other potential hazards. When you're satisfied that you've created a safe environment, let the battles begin.

ADVENTURE TIME

What kind of pillow fight are you looking to start? The impromptu method rarely fails. Grab a pillow, start swinging, and encourage everyone else to do the same thing.

Another option is to post signs around your house, announcing the time and location of the pillow fight and encouraging participants to dress in comfortable clothes and bring their favorite pillows to the brawl. (That's your cue to show up with a giant body pillow or couch cushion.)

Set a tone of playfulness for your battle. If things get too aggressive, you'll lose the spirit of fun. Take turns targeting one another so that no one feels picked on.

THAT REMINDS ME

Say something like this: *Wouldn't it be fun if, when someone makes you mad or does something to hurt you, you could challenge that person to a pillow fight? That way neither one of you would actually get hurt.*

Share a time when someone said or did something that hurt you. Invite other family members to share similar stories. Talk about whether a pillow fight would or wouldn't have been a satisfying way to resolve those conflicts.

Say something like this: *Unfortunately, it's hard to have conflict without someone getting hurt.*

FAMILY DEVOTIONS

Point out that the Bible is filled with stories of conflict and people getting hurt. Many of the stories involve families. Cain got angry with his brother Abel and killed him. Jacob tricked his older brother Esau out of his inheritance and then spent most of his life on the run from Esau. Joseph's brothers sold him into slavery.

Yet no one faced more conflict or experienced more pain than Jesus. His enemies accused Him of breaking religious laws.

They said He was possessed by a demon. They stirred people's anger against Him. They arrested Him, made false accusations against Him, beat Him, nailed Him to a cross, and left Him to die. And while He suffered, they made fun of Him.

Say something like this: *Before He died, Jesus had one final chance to address the enemies who had caused Him so much pain. What did He say?* If no one knows the answer, ask someone to read Luke 23:34 ("Father, forgive them, for they do not know what they are doing").

Ask, *What happens to conflict when you forgive someone?* If no one else mentions it, point out that when we forgive, we put the conflict in God's hands.

Say something like this: *Forgiveness takes care of the conflict on the inside. But what about the outside? What's the best way to respond to someone who tries to stir up conflict?*

Have someone read Proverbs 15:1 ("A gentle answer turns away wrath, but a harsh word stirs up anger"). Ask, *What does God want us to do when people make us mad or try to hurt us?*

Pray together, thanking God for forgiving us and for giving us a way to deal with conflict that honors Him. Ask Him to give your family members wisdom and strength to deal with the conflict they face.

LANGUAGE OF THE DAY

You can make this activity especially memorable for a family member whose primary love language is Physical Touch. Drop the pillows and start a playful wrestling session. One option is for everyone else to pile (safely) on top of that person. Another option is for everyone else to swing that person by their arms and legs and launch them into a pile of pillows.

HOW MANY CAN YOU FIT?

7

Test your family's spatial skills (and perhaps your claustrophobia) by seeing how many family members you can squeeze into a variety of small areas.

GETTING READY

The only preparation you'll need to do is to scout locations for these quick mini-adventures. The areas that will work will depend on the number and size of the people in your family. If your immediate family is very small, you may need to recruit some extended family members for this activity.

ADVENTURE TIME

Decades ago, bored college students used to try to set records for the most people crammed into a Volkswagen Bug or a phone booth or a dorm room. Here's an opportunity to rework this blast from the past as a family adventure.

This adventure will work especially well if you have a large family, but it can be tweaked to fit any size clan. The object of the adventure is simple: to see how many people you can fit in a variety of small places.

For example, how many family members can you fit in the back seat of a compact car—while still being able to close all the car doors? How many can you fit in your pantry or in the smallest closet in your house—while still being able to close the door? How many can you fit on the bottom step of your staircase—with no one touching the floor or any other step? How many can you fit on a single sidewalk square—with no one touching the ground anywhere outside the square?

You can approach these adventures with a sardine strategy—that is, simply cramming as many people as you can side-by-side into (or onto) a given space. Or you can approach it with an engineering strategy—that is, finding ways to manipulate yourselves in order to allow for maximum capacity. For example, in the "bottom step" challenge, each person standing on the step could have another person on his or her shoulders—and could also be gripping the hand of yet another person who has one foot on the step and is leaning out at a 45-degree angle.

However you choose to approach these adventures, it might be worth taking pictures and video of your efforts.

THAT REMINDS ME

Talk about some "tight" situations you've been in. For example, perhaps you grew up in a small house with one bathroom that everyone had to share. Or perhaps you had to sleep in a crowded tent during a camping trip. Or perhaps you had to crawl through a narrow tunnel. Encourage your family members to share their own stories of tight squeezes. Talk about whether any of you have ever experienced a full-blown claustrophobic reaction. If so, what was it like? How, if at all, does the incident affect you today?

Talk about your personal preferences when it comes to personal space. Which of your family members are energized by being in close contact with one another? Which ones prefer more solitude?

FAMILY DEVOTIONS

Say something like this: *One day when Jesus was visiting someone's house, so many people came to hear Him that the entire house filled up. People were packed in tight, just like we were in some of our challenges. No one else could get into the house. That was bad news for a paralyzed man whose friends had carried him on a mat to see and be healed by Jesus.*

Have someone read Luke 5:19. In the passage, the paralyzed man's four friends carry him to the top of the house, cut a hole in the roof and lower him down to Jesus. Jesus first forgives the paralyzed man's sins and then heals him.

Have someone read Luke 5:20 ("When Jesus saw their faith, he said, 'Friend, your sins are forgiven'"). Point out that it was the friends' faith that moved Jesus. Spend a few minutes talking about how you and your family can bring your friends to Jesus.

Pray together, praising God for His love and healing power and thanking Him for the friends who care deeply about you and your family. Ask Him to help you recognize and take advantage of opportunities to do meaningful things for others, like the friends in the Bible story.

LANGUAGE OF THE DAY

The physical closeness required of this adventure will automatically appeal to someone whose primary love language is Physical Touch. You can heighten the experience by instructing your family members to lift, hug, or lie on top of this person as you all try to squeeze into or onto a particular space.

TO NEXT ADVENTURE

BOWLING WITH A TWIST

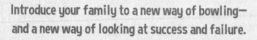

8

Introduce your family to a new way of bowling—
and a new way of looking at success and failure.

GETTING READY

Create and print out a customized scorepad for
your bowling game, one that takes into account the
unique scoring rules of this adventure. You may also
want to have a calculator handy, since you won't
have the luxury of automatic scoring.

If you want to go the extra mile, you could have
matching bowling shirts made with your family's
name or the design of your choice prominently
displayed.

ADVENTURE TIME

It's hard to compete in bowling if you're too small
to roll a ball hard and straight. One way to make up

for that is to use bumpers, which you'll need to do with this adventure. Here's another way to level the playing field (or, more appropriately, the bowling alley) so that everyone can enjoy the competition. Before you head to the bowling alley, come up with a list of "bonus opportunities," as well as a point value for each one. For example, you might award . . .

- ▶ 10 bonus points for knocking down only one pin with a single roll

- ▶ 15 bonus points for rolling a ball between two pins without knocking either down

- ▶ 20 bonus points for creating a split with your first ball

- ▶ 2x the points if your ball hits both bumpers before it hits the pins

Your goal is to create a scoring system that actually rewards things that are considered "fails" in traditional bowling.

THAT REMINDS ME

After bowling with a twist, treat your family to some "ice cream with a twist" (soft-serve) and talk about your experience. Point out that our culture has a very narrow view of success and failure. If you don't score more points than your opponent, if you don't gain acceptance right away, if you don't figure out a solution on your first attempt, some people may call you a failure.

Talk about a time when you failed at something—or at least felt like a failure. What were the circumstances? How did people react to you? How did you feel about yourself?

Point out that one way to change people's feelings about failure is to change the way we define success. The person who "won" your bowling-with-a-twist adventure may not have been the person with the highest actual score, which is the traditional view of success. Likewise, a person who fails more often than others may ultimately be more successful than others, especially if that person is gaining valuable wisdom from his or her failures.

Some of the greatest inventors and scientists in history failed more than most people—because they *tried* more often than most people. And some of the important people in history —including Abraham Lincoln and the apostle Peter—used their early failures as extra motivation to succeed.

FAMILY DEVOTIONS

Explain that on the night Jesus was arrested—before His disciples knew what was getting ready to happen—He predicted that they would all desert Him. Peter, one of Jesus' closest friends, refused to believe Him.

Have someone read Matthew 26:33–35. In the passage, Jesus tells Peter that before the night is over, Peter will disown Him three times. Yet Peter still refuses to believe that He's capable of disowning Jesus.

Explain that after Jesus was arrested, Peter followed Him to the place where He was put on trial and waited outside. Have someone read Matthew 26:69–75. In the passage, Peter disowns Jesus three times, just as Jesus had predicted. Peter is so ashamed of failing to stand by Jesus that he goes away and weeps bitterly.

Emphasize that this was not the end of Peter's story. After Jesus' resurrection, Peter became one of Jesus' boldest followers.

He learned from his failure and never again disowned Jesus—
even when he was arrested and crucified.

LANGUAGE OF THE DAY

Someone whose primary love language is Words
of Affirmation would get extra benefit from your
discussion of success and failure if you recall a
time when he or she overcame failure. Don't dwell on the failure
too much, especially if it's still a sensitive subject. Instead, affirm
your loved one for his or her handling of the failure—and for
his or her more recent successes.

TO NEXT ADVENTURE

LIBRARY SCAVENGER HUNT

9

Have some fun at your local library with a scavenger hunt. Hand out a list of things to find and set a time limit for the adventure. The one who finds or completes the most items on the list is the winner.

GETTING READY

Visit the library ahead of your adventure. Talk to a librarian about your plans. He or she may be able to recommend (a) items to add to your list, (b) a time when there are interesting programs and activities scheduled—things you might incorporate into your hunt, or (c) a time when the library generally isn't busy so that you can avoid crowds.

ADVENTURE TIME

Your list of items will depend on the ages of your kids and the resources available in your library. Here are some ideas to get you started:

- Find a book that has more than ten words in its title.

- Find out why library books have numbers on them.

- Find a book that has a pyramid on the cover.

- Find a book that has four or more animals on its cover.

- Find a book written by someone who has the same first name or initials as you.

- Help a library worker return a book to its shelf.

- Find a book about your favorite hobby.

- Find your favorite movie in the DVD section.

- Get a selfie with a librarian.

THAT REMINDS ME

When the hunt is over, find a study room or an area outside the library where you can talk. Congratulate the winner of your scavenger hunt and discuss the interesting things that happened or the unexpected things you found while you were searching.

Point out that being in a library reminds you of some of your favorite books. Summarize a few of them and talk about why they mean so much to you. Encourage everyone else to talk about his or her favorite book(s).

You might also talk about what you would each like and dislike about working at a library. Take a look, too, at some of the upcoming activities at the library and discuss which ones might be interesting for your family.

FAMILY DEVOTIONS

Start with this question: *What does a good book do for you?*
Encourage everyone in your family to offer a response. If
responses are slow in coming, throw out some of the following
ideas to get the ideas flowing.

- ▸ A good book makes you temporarily forget your
  problems.

- ▸ A good book introduces you to people and places
  you've never encountered before.

- ▸ A good book makes you laugh or cry, but ultimately
  leaves you reflecting on your life and feeling inspired.

- ▸ A good book helps you understand yourself and
  how you can become a better person.

Hold up a Bible and ask, *What does* this *book do for you?*
Again, encourage everyone to offer a response. Depending on
your kids' ages and their familiarity with Scripture, answers may
range from "It teaches us about Jesus" to "It shows us how God
works in the lives of His people" to "It tells us what we should
and shouldn't do."

Read together Psalm 119:105 ("Your word is a lamp for my
feet, a light on my path"). Talk about how God's Word shows
us His path—the way that is the best for our lives. Point out
that if we ever feel lost or don't know what to do, the Bible can
give us direction.

Use the following questions as needed to guide your discussion of the passage:

- ▶ When was the last time you used God's Word to help you decide what to do?

- ▶ Why is it so tempting to choose our own path?

- ▶ How could God's Word show you the right path in a difficult situation at school?

Pray together, thanking God for His Word and all that it does for us. Ask Him to guide your family as you study the Bible together and to give you the wisdom you need to apply its teachings to your daily lives.

LANGUAGE OF THE DAY

You can make this day especially meaningful for a family member whose primary love language is Acts of Service. Before you head to the library, fill out an index card about that family member. On one side of the card, list as many of his or her characteristics and interests as you can think of. On the other side, list his or her favorite books, movies, and TV shows.

Give the card to a librarian and ask them to make book recommendations for your family member, based on the information on the card. Before you leave the library, check out some of the recommended books for your family member to enjoy.

TO NEXT ADVENTURE

SPEED GAMING

10

Why play just one board or card game when you can play a half dozen or more in the same amount of time? Welcome to gaming in the fast lane.

GETTING READY

The object is to sample as many different games as you can in the span of an afternoon or evening. To make the transition from one game to the next as smooth as possible, you'll need to do some prep work beforehand. In order to make sure that everyone understands how to play each game—and what the abbreviated rules are—you may want to write out the basic instructions on index cards beforehand. Any prep work you can do for individual games would also be helpful, too. If, for example, you're playing Monopoly, make sure you have the money sorted beforehand.

ADVENTURE TIME

Gather your family around a table for a game night unlike any other. You'll need several board or card games, preferably ones that are familiar to your family. Since your goal is to play—and finish—as many games as possible, you'll need to amend the game play and rules.

Here are some ideas to get you started:

▶ Monopoly—Everyone gets $400. The person who buys Boardwalk wins.

▶ Scrabble—The person with the highest score after one round wins.

▶ Trivial Pursuit—The first person to get a wedge wins.

▶ Uno—The person with the low score after one hand wins.

▶ Hearts—The person with the low score after one hand wins.

▶ War—The person with the most cards after five turns wins.

▶ Yahtzee—The first person to roll a large straight wins.

▶ Sorry—The first person to move one pawn around the board wins.

▶ Hungry Hungry Hippo—The person who eats the most marbles in one round wins.

▶ Cranium Whoonu—The person who picks the Whoozit's favorite thing wins.

▶ Candyland—Mark a random spot on the board. The first person to reach that spot wins.

If you want to add a more competitive element to the adventure, keep track of who wins each abbreviated game and award a prize to the person who wins the most games.

THAT REMINDS ME

Ask your family to imagine what life would be like if people approached it like Speed Gaming. Encourage everyone to throw out some ideas. For example, what if school ended after first period? What if your workday ended after you helped your first customer, client, or patient? What if basketball games ended after the first basket was scored—or football games ended after the first touchdown or field goal was scored? What if a movie ended after the first scene?

Suggest that life probably wouldn't be very satisfying or fulfilling under those conditions. You wouldn't have time to do what you needed to do. You wouldn't feel as though you were fully experiencing anything. Things would be chaotic and crazy.

Point out that sometimes family life seems like that.

FAMILY DEVOTIONS

Summarize the story of Jesus' visit to the home of Mary and Martha. While Martha rushed here and there, busily serving her guests, Mary sat at Jesus' feet and listened to Him teach.

Ask, *When Martha complained to Jesus that Mary wasn't rushing around with her, what did Jesus tell her?* Have someone read the answer in Luke 10:41–42 ("Martha, Martha, you are worried and upset about many things, but few things are needed—or indeed only one. Mary has chosen what is better, and it will not be taken away from her.").

Say something like this: *We do a lot of rushing around in our family, don't we?* List just a few of the things in which your family members are involved, including jobs, sports, hobbies, and volunteer work. *Sometimes it seems as though there's not enough time to savor our time together because we're always rushing on to the next thing—just as we did with these games.*

Ask, *What can we learn from Mary when it comes to making time for what's important?* Discuss some ideas for setting aside and guarding family time. Depending on your schedule, that may involve dinner together two or three nights a week, breakfast on Saturday morning, or a Friday night pizza and movie routine. Whatever your schedule allows, agree as a family to honor that time and make it a priority.

Pray together, thanking God for the many opportunities that are available to your family. Ask Him to give you wisdom in choosing which commitments to honor and which ones to sacrifice for the sake of family time.

LANGUAGE OF THE DAY

If Quality Time is the primary love language of someone in your family, you can make this adventure extra special by thinking about more than competition. Some of the games you choose will likely have special meaning to your family. Perhaps there's one you play on vacation or one that you played with a loved one who's no longer around. Spend some quality time reliving those memories while you play. Encourage everyone to join in the conversation.

TO NEXT ADVENTURE

SOMETHING BLUE

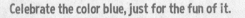

Celebrate the color blue, just for the fun of it.

11

GETTING READY

The theme of your all-day family adventure is blue. The question is, how many blue-related places and events can you find in your area? Are there any restaurants, stores, parks, or places of interest that have "Blue" in their name? With a little research and investigation, you may discover some interesting places to visit.

For extra credit, make a playlist of songs with "Blue" in the title: "Blue Suede Shoes," "Blue Eyes Crying in the Rain," "Rhapsody in Blue," "Blue Moon," "Mr. Blue Sky," to name just a few. A quick search of your favorite streaming service should yield dozens more. Choose songs from each of your family members' favorite genres.

ADVENTURE TIME

And now for something completely random. Announce to your family that you will be celebrating the color blue for an entire day. You don't need any more rhyme or reason than that. Anything goes, as long it involves something blue.

For breakfast, you might serve blueberry pancakes. For lunch, blue macaroni and cheese (courtesy of a few drops of food coloring). For dinner, chicken cordon . . . bleu?

Dress in blue clothes for the day. If the mood strikes you, paint your faces and color your hair blue.

The blue activities you choose to engage in will depend on the ages and interests of your family members, as well as the time of year. One option is to visit local shops, restaurants, parks, or places of interest that have "blue" in their name. Another option is to plant blue flowers in your garden. Still another is to color pictures in a coloring book using only blue crayons (of which there are several different shades).

Watch a movie with "Blue" in the title. Go on a scavenger hunt for blue things around your neighborhood.

THAT REMINDS ME

Throughout the day, engage your family in conversations that have to do with the color blue. For example, you might throw out discussion-starters such as

▶ Where does blue rank on the list of your favorite colors?

▶ What shade of blue is your favorite?

▶ Why do you think blue is traditionally associated with boys?

Throughout the day, keep a running list of your family's favorite blue things—which may include the ocean, the sky, robin eggs, and bluebirds.

FAMILY DEVOTIONS

Point out that when it comes to emotions, the color blue is closely associated with sadness and depression. Open up about times when you've struggled with sadness or depression and encourage your family members to do the same.

Say something like this: *The good news is that God cares deeply about us.* Hold up your Bible. *Some of the most famous people in His Word struggled with sadness and depression. We can find their stories and struggles in the pages of the Bible. We can also find words of wisdom and comfort to draw on as we work through our own blue times.*

Have someone read Psalm 34:17–18 ("The righteous cry out, and the LORD hears them; he delivers them from all their troubles. The LORD is close to the brokenhearted and saves those who are crushed in spirit"). Point out that David, the man who wrote these words, understood God better than most people do. He had experienced God's closeness and healing firsthand.

Pray together, thanking God for the opportunity to have fun together as a family. Praise Him for His compassion and His willingness to stand close to us when we're hurting. Ask Him to work in the lives of your family members who struggle with sadness and depression, that you may always feel His presence.

LANGUAGE OF THE DAY

A blue ribbon would be just what the doctor ordered for someone whose primary love language is Words of Affirmation. At the end of your Blue Day, award a blue ribbon to your Words of Affirmation family member for a recent accomplishment or an impressive character trait that you see in him or her. You can even create unique blue ribbons for each person. The more specific you are about what the ribbon is for, the more meaningful it will be to your family member.

TO NEXT ADVENTURE

STEALTH SERVICE

Spend a day performing acts of kindness, without drawing attention to yourselves.

12

GETTING READY

To make the most of your day, it's best to have a working agenda—a list of things you would like to do and a general timeline of when you will do them. A week or two before your adventure, post a list in your house and encourage each of your family members to write down ideas for acts of kindness you can perform as a family. Select the ideas—preferably at least one from each family member—that best lend themselves to your day-long adventure for your working agenda.

Of course, while you're following your agenda, you'll want to keep your eyes open for spontaneous acts of kindness you can perform.

ADVENTURE TIME

Your goal is to see how many meaningful acts of kindness your family can perform in one day. The acts you choose and the way you perform them will depend upon your family, your setting, and your circumstances.

The possibilities are limitless. You could rake leaves for an elderly neighbor (if you plan your adventure in autumn). You could shovel snow for the same neighbor (if you plan it in winter). You could prepare a care package for a soldier stationed overseas. You could deliver a meal for a family dealing with a health crisis. You could clean up a section of a local park, creek, or beach. You could volunteer to babysit for an hour or so—long enough for a frazzled parent to run some errands or enjoy a quick lunch with a friend. (For maximum benefit, you may need to schedule this in advance.)

Whatever you do, keep it low-key. Don't call attention to your acts of kindness.

THAT REMINDS ME

Ask, *What's the nicest or most helpful thing anyone has ever done for you?* Be prepared to break the ice by sharing your own story of someone who helped you in a profound way. Talk about how it feels when people take the time to focus on *your* needs. Encourage your family members to share their own stories.

FAMILY DEVOTIONS

Have someone read 1 John 4:19 ("We love because He first loved us"). Point out that the reason we're able to show love and concern for others is that God first showed love and concern for us. That's why our responsibility, as God's people, is to give all glory and honor to Him.

Have someone read Matthew 6:3–4 ("But when you give to the needy, do not let your left hand know what your right hand is doing, so that your giving may be in secret. Then your Father, who sees what is done in secret, will reward you"). Ask, *What happens when we tell others about something kind that we've done—or when we post it on social media?* If no one else mentions it, point out that *we* get attention for it. People tell us how great *we* are.

Ask, *What happens when we do random acts of kindness without anyone knowing?* If no one else mentions it, suggest that many people may see them as answers to prayer and give God the glory for them.

Pray together, thanking God for loving us and for giving us the opportunity to show love to others. Ask Him to bless your efforts to do random acts of kindness so that He will be glorified in the lives of others.

LANGUAGE OF THE DAY

Point out that being stealthy about your random acts of kindness doesn't mean you can never talk about them. If Words of Affirmation is the primary love language of someone in your family, single them out for praise at the end of your adventure. Talk about how proud you are of the servant's heart that beats within their chest. Be specific in mentioning ways that they made someone's day better or easier.

TO NEXT ADVENTURE

FOSTER A PET

Make arrangements with a local shelter to temporarily care for an animal in need. If this is not possible or practical, other options could be to get a goldfish or an ant farm.

13

GETTING READY

This adventure will require a bit of preparation. Specifically, you'll need to animal-proof your house. Never underestimate the ability of cats and dogs to get into places where they're not supposed to be or to get a hold of things they're not supposed to have. Look carefully at the places where you will be sheltering the animal. Remove anything that can be destroyed or anything that might cause harm to your temporary guest. The local shelter where you pick up your foster pet will likely address this issue in more detail.

If you've never fostered before, you'll also need to fill out the necessary paperwork and pass a background check before you take an animal home. If you want to avoid delays on the day of pickup, you'll need to complete these steps ahead of time.

ADVENTURE TIME

Fostering a pet is a big, rewarding responsibility. Before you agree to do it, you'll need to make sure that everyone in your family is on board and willing to help. Set up a rotating job schedule that includes feeding, cleaning, walking, and any other foster responsibility. Make sure that everyone has a part in caring for your furry visitor.

Make sure, too, that you know what you're getting into. If a shelter is overcrowded, you may be able to choose whether you want a cat or dog, young or old, healthy or unhealthy. If it's an emergency situation, you may be asked to take an animal that needs special care.

Explain to your family that this adventure will last longer than a day. In fact, it may be open-ended.

 ## THAT REMINDS ME

Spend some time talking about the pets you had when you were growing up. What was the name of your favorite pet? Where did the name come from? How old were you when you got them? How old were you when they died? What was your pet's personality like? What did they like to do? If you have any pictures of your pet, this would be a great time to show them.

Ask each of your family members what kind of pet, if any, they would like to have and why. After everyone has had a chance to share, talk about the best things and the worst things about having a pet. The best things might include snuggling, companionship, and playfulness. The worst things might include having to clean up after an animal, the lack of freedom that comes with pet ownership, and the expenses of feeding and caring for pets.

FAMILY DEVOTIONS

Say something like this: *The connection between humans and animals stretches all the way back to creation.* Have someone read Genesis 2:19 ("Now the LORD God had formed out of the ground all the wild animals and all the birds in the sky. He brought them to the man to see what he would name them; and whatever the man called each living creature, that was its name").

Have someone read Psalm 136:25 ("He gives food to every creature. His love endures forever"). Say something like this: *The Bible says that we are created in God's image. How does our care for animals reflect God's image?* If no one else mentions it, point out that as the Creator and Sustainer of the universe, God cares deeply for all living creatures. He takes care of them. When we care for His creatures, we reflect His image.

Have someone read Proverbs 12:10 ("The righteous care for the needs of their animals, but the kindest acts of the wicked are cruel"). Ask, *Why do you think Solomon, the man who wrote this proverb, connected taking care of animals with being righteous?* If no one else mentions it, point out that it reveals how much importance God places on His animal creation.

Pray together, praising God for the beauty and noble qualities found in the animals He created. Ask Him to give your family wisdom, patience, and endurance as you foster a pet in your home.

LANGUAGE OF THE DAY

If Acts of Service is the primary love language of someone in your family, your pet-fostering adventure will give you an opportunity to do something meaningful for them. On a day when they are overwhelmed by schoolwork, a hectic work or sports schedule, and other responsibilities, take their turn in caring for your foster pet.

TO NEXT ADVENTURE

VOLUNTEER DAY

Spend a day helping an organization that helps people in need.

14

GETTING READY

This adventure is different from Stealth Service (see pages 55–58). This is about volunteering with an organized group in order to assist others. Help your kids understand the power of organized responses to suffering and need. Explain that organizations, because of their size, can do things that individuals can't. Along those same lines, help your kids understand that individual efforts are what make up organizations. That's why your family adventure is going to involve helping an organization meet the needs of hurting people.

Talk to nonprofits and outreach ministries in your area. Find out what your family can do to help and then schedule times to volunteer. This is an all-day adventure, so if you can coordinate schedules—and if your family has the stamina—you may be able to volunteer for more than one organization in a day.

ADVENTURE TIME

Organizations such as Feed My Starving Children offer organized service opportunities for families and other groups. Feed My Starving Children will put you to work packing boxes of food that will be distributed to needy people in developing countries. Some veterans' organizations offer the opportunity to prepare care packages for soldiers stationed overseas.

Another option is to volunteer at a local food pantry, preparing and serving food. This will allow you to interact with the people you serve. Another face-to-face  option is to volunteer with a homeless outreach that allows you to distribute food, clothes, blankets, and other essentials to people on the street. You might also check with the outreach ministry at your church to see if there are any volunteer opportunities available there.

The best-case scenario is that you find an organization or ministry that resonates especially powerfully with your family. It would be great if you find a service opportunity that continues long after your day of adventure has ended.

THAT REMINDS ME

Spend some time talking about different scenarios that can cause a person's—or a family's—circumstances to change dramatically. An unexpected pregnancy. A divorce or the abandonment of a spouse. A medical emergency. The loss of a job. A fire. A natural disaster. An addiction. All of these things can create needs that people just can't meet on their own. They need help. They need an organization to turn to.

If you or anyone you know has ever been on the receiving end of organizational assistance, talk about the experience. What was the immediate impact? What long-term effects did it have, spiritually speaking? How did it change opinions about the goodness and generosity of others?

If you've gone on a mission trip, talk about your experience. What were the people to whom you ministered like? What were their living conditions and challenges? What impact do you think your ministry had? What did you take away from the experience?

FAMILY DEVOTIONS

Have your family members take turns reading Matthew 25:31–46. In the passage, Jesus identifies so closely with the outcasts of society—the hungry, the thirsty, the sick, strangers with nowhere to go, people with tattered clothes, prisoners—that He says if we do things to help them, we're actually helping Him. Likewise, if we fail to help those in need, it's the same as failing to help Jesus.

Ask, *Why do you think Jesus wants people to associate Him with people who get overlooked and mistreated?* If no one else mentions it, point out that when He was on earth, those were the people He helped. When He went back to heaven, He left His followers in charge of caring for them.

What are some things that keep people from helping those who are hungry, thirsty, sick, strangers, poor, or prisoners? If no one else mentions it, point out that some people feel helpless themselves and don't know what to do. Some people are too focused on their own problems. Some people are scared to get involved.

What did we accomplish today? If no one else mentions it, point out that whatever you did for someone in need, you did for Jesus.

LANGUAGE OF THE DAY

If Receiving Gifts is the primary love language of someone in your family, you can give them a powerful reminder of your volunteer adventure. Frame a small photo of someone who was helped by your work and present it to them.

TO NEXT ADVENTURE

BIKE WASH & TUNE-UP CENTER

Help the kids in your neighborhood get their bikes looking good and running well.

15

GETTING READY

You'll need to create a tune-up center and wash area in your yard. For the tune-up center, you'll need some bike tools and an air pump. (If you're unfamiliar with the basics of bike maintenance, you might also want to enlist the assistance of a cycling enthusiast.) For the wash area, you'll need a hose, a bucket of soapy water, a few sponges, and some towels.

In advance of your adventure, post signs around your neighborhood, inviting kids to bring their bicycles—and tricycles—to your house for a free wash and tune-up. You might also decorate your yard with balloons and streamers to get attention.

ADVENTURE TIME

One way to approach this adventure is with an assembly line. For example, kids will bring their bicycles first to the tune-up center, where the tire pressure and brakes are checked, the seat is adjusted, and the nuts and bolts of the frame are tightened. From there, they will proceed to the wash area, where the bike is scrubbed clean, rinsed, and dried.

Each family member will man one or more of the stations. Make sure that you switch jobs frequently so that no one gets bored or overworked. You'll also want to build plenty of time into your afternoon for water fights and wet-sponge tosses.

If you really want to get ambitious, you could offer refreshments to your customers while they wait. Your goal is to have fun as a family while you provide a service to the kids in your neighborhood.

THAT REMINDS ME

If you have a lull in your service schedule, talk about the bike you had when you were a kid. Was it a source of pride or embarrassment for you? How did it compare to your friends' bikes? Where did you ride it? Were you a daredevil or a cautious rider? What did your bike mean to you? If you have any old pictures of your bike, bring them out.

If you don't have a lot of bike nostalgia, try a different conversation starter. Ask, *What's the best thing about being a kid?* Encourage each of your family members to offer an answer. Responses may range from "Not having to worry about adult things" to "Having summers off."

Let that lead to the inevitable follow-up question, *What's the worst thing about being a kid?* Again, encourage everyone to weigh in with an opinion. Responses may range from "Getting bossed around by adults" to "Having to go to school all day."

FAMILY DEVOTIONS

Point out that no matter how bad things are now for kids, they were a lot worse in Jesus' day. Have someone read Matthew 19:13–15. Ask, *Why do you think Jesus' disciples tried to keep children away from Jesus?* If no one else mentions it, suggest that they may have believed that Jesus had more important things to do than entertain children.

Say something like this: *Not only did Jesus welcome children, He held them up as examples.* Have someone read Matthew 18:1–5. In the passage, Jesus' disciples ask Him who will be greatest in the kingdom of God. Jesus calls a child to Himself and tells them that they can't be great in God's eyes unless they make themselves as humble as children.

Ask, *What is it about children that the Lord wants us to model?* If no one else mentions it, point out that children are dependent on their parents and obedient to them. They don't try to act more important than they are. That's the way God wants His people to be.

LANGUAGE OF THE DAY

If Acts of Service is the primary love language of one of your family members—and if that person owns a bike—you could do something meaningful for them by putting extra effort into cleaning and tuning up their bike.

TO NEXT ADVENTURE

THAT'S NOT HOW THE STORY ENDS

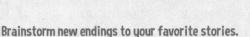

Brainstorm new endings to your favorite stories.

16

GETTING READY

This quick adventure requires some creativity. To facilitate your family's creative impulses, prepare a list of stories that are familiar to everyone in your family. They may be fairy tales, movie plots, or favorite bedtime stories. Next to each story on the list, write a one- or two-sentence summary of an "alternate ending" to the story, one that takes it in a whole new direction. For example, what if the three bears called the police to report a home invasion and had Goldilocks arrested? What if Dorothy brought the Scarecrow, Tin Man, and Cowardly Lion back to Kansas with her at the end of *The Wizard of Oz*? What if Cinderella sprained her foot running down the castle stairs and the swelling caused the glass slipper not to fit?

Share these alternate endings to give your family members an idea of what you're looking for.

ADVENTURE TIME

Take turns sharing your favorite stories from books, movies, and TV shows. Give a brief recap of how the story actually ends. Then offer your own ending—one that's happier, stranger, or more interesting. Your ending may turn a minor character into a heroine or turn a tragic death into nothing more than a close call.

The aim of this adventure is to inspire creativity by turning passive readers and viewers into active ones. You're encouraging your kids to interact with what they watch and read—to think critically about it. You're encouraging them to develop their own creative voice.

THAT REMINDS ME

Talk about some real-life "alternate endings" you've experienced—that is, times when you thought a situation would turn out one way, but were surprised when it turned out another way. Perhaps you were sent home for fighting at school, but instead of getting in trouble with your parents you were praised for standing up to a bully.

Try to keep the stories positive, with endings that turned out better than expected. Your goal is to help your kids understand that dread, fear, and worry are often misplaced emotions. If we can't see how something good ultimately can come from something that seems bad, we're not looking at it from the right perspective. We're not taking into account how God can change the ending.

FAMILY DEVOTIONS

Summarize the story of Daniel, the young man in the Old Testament who was taken captive when Babylon conquered Israel. Because Daniel was well-educated and well-trained, the king of Babylon put him to work in his court as an adviser. Because God seemed to bless everything Daniel did, the king's other advisers got jealous.

They convinced the king to pass a law that made it illegal to pray to anyone but the king. The jealous advisers knew that Daniel would be trapped because he prayed to God every day. So the next time Daniel prayed, they had him arrested. The king was upset because he didn't realize that was going to happen. But he couldn't go against his own law.

Have someone read Daniel 6:1–18. Ask, *What was Daniel's punishment for praying to God?* Point out that the lions were starved on purpose so that they would kill and eat anything—or anyone—that was thrown into their pit.

Ask, *Based on what you know about starving lions, how would you expect Daniel's story to end?* After you've received a response or two, have someone read Daniel 6:19–23. Point out that God can change any story.

Pray together, thanking God for the example of Daniel and others in the Bible who stayed faithful to Him and were rewarded in incredible ways. Ask Him to give you and your family the strength and courage to follow their examples.

LANGUAGE OF THE DAY

This adventure lends itself nicely to someone whose primary love language is Receiving Gifts. Buy a copy of one of your favorite books—preferably one that has a triumphant or unexpectedly happy ending. Inscribe the book to your family member, making note of the date, the occasion, and why the book is meaningful to you. When the time is right, present the book to your family member.

TO NEXT ADVENTURE

CREATE A FAMILY LIP-SYNC VIDEO

Choreograph a performance to one of your favorite songs and record it for posterity.

17

GETTING READY

Watch a few viral lip-sync videos together to get an idea of what you want to do. Choose a song that you all like—one that's easy to lip-sync and fun to perform. You might also want to choose a theme for your video. Because your entire family will be in front of the camera performing, you'll need to recruit a camera operator. You may also want to find a director or choreographer to make the shoot run smoothly.

ADVENTURE TIME

Before you begin shooting, you may find it helpful to plot out your video in detail. Lay out your set and decorate it according to your theme. Decide who will "sing" each part. If you use a moving camera, get your timing down so that you know when the camera will reach a certain point, and so on.

Practice the routine enough times to get it down, but don't overdo it. In the balance between creating something good enough to go viral and just having fun as a family, err on the side of having fun as a family.

Decide whether you want to capture the performance in one continuous shot or shoot it scene-by-scene and then edit the scenes together later. Make sure that you have the song on your playlist—and that you have speakers handy—so that you can play it while you film.

When your video is done, invite friends and family over for a viewing party. And if all of your family members are okay with the idea, post it on social media for others to enjoy.

THAT REMINDS ME

Talk about things you've done in the past that involved the participation of several different people. If you were in marching band, talk about the hours of practice and formation drills. If you were on a basketball team, talk about the complex plays you ran that depended on all five players moving as one. If you worked at a restaurant, talk about how servers and kitchen staff worked together during busy times.

Suggest that practice, familiarity, and dependability are the keys to smoothness. Anytime you repeat something over and over again, you get better at it. At the same time, the longer you're around a group of people, the better you get at anticipating their moves and coordinating yours with theirs. Once you know someone can be trusted to do her thing, it frees you to do yours.

FAMILY DEVOTIONS

Say something like this: *Our ability to work together as a group— to accomplish things that one person working alone couldn't do— comes from God. He designed us to fit together with others.*

Have your family members take turns reading 1 Corinthians 12:12–26. In the passage, the apostle Paul explains that every believer is part of the body of Christ. As with a human body, each part has a function, a responsibility that helps the entire body.

Ask, *Why is it important for each of us to use our God-given gifts in the body of Christ?* If no one else mentions it, point out that every part of the body is necessary. If one person chooses not to function, the rest of the body suffers in ways we can't always see. Other people have to do more to make up for the absence, which makes them less effective at fulfilling their own responsibilities. The result is that the body of Christ isn't as effective as it could be. You might want to connect this question to your lip-sync video. If one of you didn't do what you were supposed to do, the entire production would have suffered.

Talk about the specific gifts your family members could put to use in your church or in other areas of Christian ministry.

LANGUAGE OF THE DAY

You can make this adventure special for someone in your family whose primary love language is Quality Time. In your video, plan one segment that features just the two of you, perhaps doing some kind of synchronized choreography. Make the most of the time you spend together, creating and practicing your moves.

TO NEXT ADVENTURE

CITIES TO EXPLORE

Your quest is simple: to see how many different cities, towns, villages, and municipalities you can visit in a single day.

18

GETTING READY

The more time you spend plotting your course, the more productive your adventure will be. Research historical, local, and pop-cultural landmarks in your vicinity. Search online for out-of-the-way (but well-reviewed) family restaurants and places of interest. Get the necessary information (business hours and location) so that you can plan your trip accordingly. Your goal is to hit each eating establishment or point of interest at just the right time. Then you can fill in your itinerary with as many other stops as possible along the way.

ADVENTURE TIME

The first thing you need to do is establish the rules for "visiting" a city or town. In order for a stop to count, the entire family has to pose for a photo in front of a sign bearing the name of the city—or in front of an identifying feature of the town. After the picture is taken, the family jumps back into the car and drives to the next city or town.

The key to a successful adventure is balance. Your kids will likely enjoy rushing in and out of the car and then hurrying to the next destination (while obeying all applicable traffic laws) to do it again. When there are sights to be savored, however, make sure you savor them. When you find places of historical significance, make sure your kids are aware of their importance. When you sit down together to eat, make sure you give yourselves time to enjoy the food—and one another's company.

If you thoroughly plot your course before you leave, you might want to create and hand out an itinerary for your kids to refer to so that they can keep track of the cities and towns.

THAT REMINDS ME

Between stops, make a list of the different states and countries each of you has visited. Encourage each family member to share his or her favorite memory of each place. Make a second list of the different states and countries you would *like* to visit and why. Talk about how much time you would like to spend in each place.

FAMILY DEVOTIONS

Say something like this: *Jesus sent His disciples on a trip kind of like this one.* Have someone read Luke 10:1–9. In the passage, Jesus sends out seventy-two of His followers, with very specific instructions.

Ask, *What were the traveling instructions the disciples had to follow?* If no one else mentions it, point out the benefits of traveling in pairs. For one thing, you would always have a companion, so you wouldn't feel lonely. You would also have a little more safety and comfort, knowing that someone has your back. Spend a little time discussing the challenges of Jesus' assignment. Point out that the disciples had to travel light and depend on strangers for hospitality. That's not an easy thing to do.

If you have your Bibles, ask everyone turn to the book of Acts. Point out that the book is filled with stories of people following Jesus' instructions in Luke 10. The apostles Peter and Paul, along with many others, traveled from city to city, telling people about Jesus and creating new churches along the way.

Say something like this: *Many of these evangelists were thrown in jail, beaten, and tortured for spreading the gospel. Yet still they traveled, preached, and taught—until the day they were put to death for telling people about Jesus.*

Talk briefly about the risks people today face when it comes to telling others about Jesus. In some places, Christians are still put in jail. In others, they are taunted, ignored, and accused of being narrow-minded or intolerant.

LANGUAGE OF THE DAY

If Receiving Gifts is the primary love language of one of your family members, create for that person a scrapbook of your adventure that includes a picture taken in every city and town. If you know ahead of time that you're going to be creating a scrapbook, make sure you take a good mix of family and solo pictures throughout the day so that you have plenty of options to choose from.

TO NEXT ADVENTURE

CAMERA ART

Give each person in your family a camera and see what develops. If you can find them, disposable cameras would work well, but any camera will do.

19

GETTING READY

Scout a variety of locations. Keep in mind that not everyone is inspired by scenes of nature or rugged landscapes. Look for some urban sites as well—or perhaps a park or some other place where crowds gather. If you have time, scout some offbeat locations as well—for example, an abandoned building or a weathered barn. The more creativity you use in choosing the sites, the better chance you'll have of inspiring creativity in your family members.

ADVENTURE TIME

If you found some disposable cameras, make sure everyone knows how to operate them. Make sure, too, that everyone understands the limited number of shots available to them. (This is especially important if your kids are used to taking an unlimited number of photos with their phones or devices.)

Give your family members their cameras and encourage them to create art or memories. Let them photograph anything they want in any manner they want. Let their artistry and eye for what's important shine through.

Explain that the purpose of this adventure is to discover how each of you sees the world—what catches your eye, what moves you, where you find beauty, what "art" looks like to you, what you believe needs to be captured in a photograph. In other words, someone looking at the photos you take should be able to learn a little about you from them.

When you're done, get the photos printed and give everyone a chance to present their work to the family. Encourage your family members to talk about what they saw that inspired them to take a particular shot.

If the adventure is a success, consider making it an annual event. If you save your kids' pictures every year, you'll have a photographic progression of their artistry or their sense of what's meaningful.

THAT REMINDS ME

Talk about some of the most creative people you've ever known. How did they express their creativity? If possible, mention examples from a wide variety of artistic endeavors. Some people express themselves through photography. Others express themselves by writing fiction or poetry. Some people write music; others sing, dance, or act. Some people build things; others bake things.

Ask your family members to talk about their favorite ways to show creativity. If you have time, encourage each family member to play a song, share a picture or video, or describe a specific expression of creativity that is meaningful to him or her.

FAMILY DEVOTIONS

Have someone read Exodus 35:31–33 ("And he [the Lord] has filled him with the Spirit of God, with wisdom, with understanding, with knowledge and with all kinds of skills—to make artistic designs for work in gold, silver and bronze, to cut and set stones, to work in wood and to engage in all kinds of artistic crafts"). Ask, *Where does our creativity come from?* If no one else mentions it, point out that creativity is a gift from God.

Have someone read Colossians 3:23 ("Whatever you do, work at it with all your heart, as working for the Lord"). Ask, *What should we do with our creativity?* If no one else mentions it, point out that we should learn to express it in meaningful ways. Ask, *How can we use our creativity to bless others?* God gave each of us a unique perspective and a unique way of expressing it. We have no way of knowing who will be moved or inspired by what we do. So when we choose *not* to express what's inside of us in a creative way, we may be depriving people of inspiration or enjoyment.

LANGUAGE OF THE DAY

You can make this activity especially meaningful for someone whose primary love language is Receiving Gifts. Choose one of that person's most prized photos, and give them the gift of having that photo professionally framed and hung in your house.

TO NEXT ADVENTURE

MIRROR GAMES

Have some fun and do some
reflecting in front of a mirror.

20

GETTING READY

For some of these games, you'll need the biggest
mirror in your house. If that mirror is in your bathroom, you may need to do some cleaning—or at
least some putting away of things on your counter—
before your adventure begins. You'll also need a few
handheld mirrors and other supplies, depending on
which activities you choose to do.

ADVENTURE TIME

Plan a series of quick games, activities, and challenges.
The only thing these ventures will have in common
is that they involve a mirror—and, ideally, some fun

and laughter. Here are a few mirror-related contests to get you started. Feel free to add your own.

- ▶ Have a race around your house. Contestants must walk backward and use a hand mirror to navigate.

- ▶ Challenge pairs to attempt a rhythmic hand-clapping game, such as Pat-A-Cake or something more complex, without the partners looking at one another. Instead, they must look sideways in the mirror.

- ▶ Instruct your family members to stand shoulder to shoulder, facing the mirror. Give each a person a toothpick. Give the person on one end a Life Saver. The challenge is to pass the Life Saver from one end to the other, using only the toothpicks. The catch is that everyone must look in the mirror the entire time.

- ▶ One of the most famous comic moments in movie history is the "mirror scene" from *Duck Soup*. Watch the scene (which runs about three minutes and is easily located with a quick online search) with your family. Then have pairs of your family members try to copy it by pretending they are mirror images of one another.

THAT REMINDS ME

Challenge your family members to rank themselves according to how much time they spend in front of a mirror every day. (To add a fun twist to your discussion, you could secretly keep track of each person's mirror time throughout the week and reveal the results of your observation here.) Give each person a chance to explain why he or she takes so much (or so little) time in front of the mirror.

Talk about what you see when you look in the mirror. Make note of how you've changed physically over the years and how you feel about it. For the sake of setting a body-positive example for your kids, embrace those changes. For example, you might mention that laugh lines are evidence of a life well-lived.

FAMILY DEVOTIONS

Have someone read 1 Corinthians 13:12 ("For now we see only a reflection as in a mirror; then we shall see face to face. Now I know in part; then I shall know fully, even as I am fully known"). Explain that the apostle Paul was talking about seeing the world from God's point of view. From a human perspective, there are a lot of tough questions we face, including . . .

▸ Why does God allow evil?

▸ Why do innocent people suffer?

▸ Why is temptation so hard to resist?

Encourage your family members to add their own questions to the list—preferably ones they have struggled with for a while. Point out that trying to answer these questions is like looking in a dark mirror. We don't have the vision we need. But the Bible promises that one day we will be face to face with Jesus, and we will have all of our questions answered.

Ask, *How do you think God feels about our questions and confusion?* If no one else mentions it, point out that God created us. He knows what makes us tick. He understands our questions and confusion. He's not offended by them; He asks us to have faith in Him—and in the fact that one day He will make everything right.

LANGUAGE OF THE DAY

This adventure offers a potent opportunity to bond with a child whose primary love language is Quality Time. Spend some time with your child studying one another's features in the mirror. Tell them who their eyes, ears, nose, smile, and hair resemble.

TO NEXT ADVENTURE

SWITCH ROOMS

Find out how the other half lives by switching bedrooms with your family members.

21

GETTING READY

If your plan is to do a temporary switch, in which each family member simply takes over someone else's room for the day—and perhaps the night— you don't need to do anything except establish the ground rules (see the "Adventure Time" section).

If, however, you want to do something a little more permanent, in which your kids *actually* trade bedrooms, you'll need to figure out the logistics of moving furniture and possessions from one room to another.

ADVENTURE TIME

As long as everyone is in agreement regarding the switch, do a temporary—or permanent—room switch. If you do a temporary switch, you could move into one child's room and your spouse could move into another child's room. If there are more than four people in your family, you might want to draw names for room assignments. Establish some ground rules for the switch. Each person is allowed to bring enough into the new room to make it his or her own (temporarily)—but not so much that it's difficult to undo later.

Each person may also designate parts of his or her room "off limits" to the new occupant. Those wishes must be honored. Discourage your kids from snooping or wreaking havoc on one another's rooms. Also, if they have possessions that they do not want to be shared during this activity, suggest they place those in the "off limits" area of the room, such as a closet.

Encourage your family members, however, to explore the areas of the room that are open to them in order to get a better understanding of the person or persons who live there. Encourage them also to make themselves comfortable in their new digs and enjoy the change of pace.

Decide whether you want to switch back before bedtime or have everyone sleep in their new arrangements.

If you make a more long-term move and allow your kids to switch furniture and everything, you may want to give them a two-week window to determine whether they really want to make it permanent or not.

THAT REMINDS ME

Describe your childhood bedroom to your family. Did it seem big or small to you? What color were the walls painted? How big was your closet? What did your bed look like? What other furniture did you have in it? Did you envy a sibling's bedroom? Did a sibling envy yours? Or were you all perfectly content with your rooms?

Suggest that it's not necessarily the *size* of a room that's important—it's the way you personalize it and make it uniquely yours. Talk about the posters, photos, and mementos that adorned your room and what they meant to you. Encourage your kids to talk about the things in their rooms that make them uniquely theirs. Talk about what a stranger could learn about each person in your family simply by looking at his or her room.

FAMILY DEVOTIONS

Say something like this: *Imagine how confused your friends would be if they came to visit. They wouldn't know where to find you. Of course, there's Someone who can never be fooled—who always knows where to find you.*

Have someone read Psalm 139:7–12. In the passage, David asks the rhetorical questions, "Where can I go from your Spirit? Where can I flee from your presence?" He realizes that if he were to go up to the heavens or down to the depths, God would be there. And if he tried to hide in the darkness, God's light would find him.

Ask, *Can you think of an example of when someone might want to get away from God?* If no one mentions it, point out that Adam and Eve tried to hide from God after they sinned (Gen. 3:8), and Jonah tried to run away from God when he didn't want to do what God commanded him (Jonah 1:1–3).

Ask, *When is it especially comforting to know that God's presence is always near?* If no one else mentions it, suggest that when we feel overlooked, forgotten, or lonely—or especially when we feel lost—it can make a big difference to know that God not only knows where we are, but is right next to us through it all.

LANGUAGE OF THE DAY

Arrange to trade rooms with a family member whose primary love language is Acts of Service. As a gift of love to him or her, spend some time organizing and cleaning the room, leaving it in much better condition than you found it in. You might also want to brainstorm some ideas with him or her for renovating the room—repainting it, getting new furniture, rearranging the closet, or anything else you can think of.

TO NEXT ADVENTURE

SHOW ME HOW TO DO THAT

Everyone is a teacher when it comes to demonstrating a special skill.

22

GETTING READY

Give your family plenty of advance notice before you embark on this adventure. Instruct everyone to choose a specific skill that he or she possesses (or something that he or she knows how to do well) to teach to the rest of the family. Explain that each person will get fifteen minutes to present a tutorial to the family.

Encourage your family members to put some time and thought into their tutorials. Discovering each person's preferred teaching style will be half the fun. Depending on the ages of your kids, you may want to lay down some ground rules that encourage polite and eager listening.

ADVENTURE TIME

One at a time, your family members will present their tutorials. Their subjects may include anything from singing a favorite song to shooting free throws to making cupcakes to getting to a certain level in a video game. Each person will get fifteen minutes to make his or her presentation. Afterward, open the floor for questions or comments.

Set some ground rules beforehand. No one is allowed to tease or laugh at the presenter or complain that they already know how to do whatever it is the presenter is teaching. Everyone must give the presenter their full attention. (Confiscate phones and devices beforehand.) Encourage everyone to be courteous, engaged, and motivated listeners.

Afterward, the audience will attempt to perform the given task based on the instruction. If you all succeed, give credit to your excellent teacher. If not, ask for further instruction and keep working on it (even after your adventure is over) until you get it right.

THAT REMINDS ME

Get your family members thinking about who their own teachers were. Ask questions such as,

▶ Who taught you how to whistle?

▶ Who taught you how to fish?

▶ Who taught you how to tie your shoes?

▶ Who taught you how to bake?

▶ Who taught you how to drive?

Encourage your family members to think of other important things people have taught them. You could then switch up the conversation and talk about skills you *wish* someone had taught you (or skills you wish someone had taught you *earlier*). If the discussion seems to be flowing, talk about what makes someone a good teacher. You may learn even more about your family members' preferred learning styles.

FAMILY DEVOTIONS

Say something like this: *God created us with a thirst for knowledge and a mind capable of absorbing all kinds of new information. Our job is to learn from those who can teach us and teach those who can learn from us.*

Have someone read Proverbs 9:9 ("Instruct the wise and they will be wiser still; teach the righteous and they will add to their learning") and Romans 12:6–7 ("We have different gifts, according to the grace given to each of us. If your gift is prophesying, then prophesy in accordance with your faith; if it is serving, then serve; if it is teaching, then teach").

Ask, *How do you know if someone has the gift of teaching?* If no one else mentions it, suggest that if you love to learn and are able to explain what you have learned to others in an engaging, easy-to-understand way, then you have the gift of teaching.

Ask, *In addition to the skill you just taught us, what knowledge, abilities, and experience do you have that other people might be able to learn from?* Be prepared to help your family members recognize what they have to offer.

LANGUAGE OF THE DAY

In conjunction with this tutorial adventure, you can have a profound impact on someone whose primary love language is Words of Affirmation with a simple request. Think of something *else* that person can do really well and ask him or her to teach you how to do it. Acknowledging the person's skill and requesting their assistance is a powerful way to affirm someone.

TO NEXT ADVENTURE

PHOTOBOMBING

Deface the photos in your house in harmless and creative ways.

23

GETTING READY

You'll need plenty of construction paper, yarn, felt, cotton balls, pipe cleaners, scissors, double-sided tape, and other craft supplies for this project. You'll also need plenty of glass cleaner to wipe down your picture frames after the adventure is over.

If you have time, you might also want to demonstrate by example. Choose a photo that hangs in your house to "deface" (see the instructions in the "Adventure Time" section). Then hang it back up and wait for your family members to notice. Seeing what you've done should get their own creative juices flowing.

ADVENTURE TIME

This adventure is really nothing more than sanctioned graffiti. Liven up the photos that hang in your house with a quick, harmless makeover, using nothing more than Sunday school craft supplies.

To be clear, you won't be decorating the photos themselves, but the glass frames that cover them. Using the supplies on hand, add mustaches, beards, wigs, fangs, eye patches, baseball caps, Santa hats, and anything else you can think of.

Keep the tone lighthearted and fun. If your kids decorate photos of one another, make sure that they don't do anything that would be upsetting or embarrassing to the other person.

THAT REMINDS ME

Ideally some of the photos you decorate should be of people outside of your immediate family—grandparents, aunts and uncles, cousins, and perhaps even more distant ancestors. That will give you the opportunity to ask, *How do you think Grandma would react if she knew we were doing this to her photo?* Talk about which of your relatives would find it funny and which ones might be offended, even though your decorations are all in good fun. If you have photos of ancestors you don't know, try to guess what their reactions would be based on their expressions in the photos.

Let that lead into a discussion of when it's appropriate to take a stand for yourself and when it's appropriate to laugh at yourself. Talk about times when people laughed at your expense in a hurtful way and times when you joined in the laughter without feeling hurt.

FAMILY DEVOTIONS

Have someone read Proverbs 17:22 ("A cheerful heart is good medicine, but a crushed spirit dries up the bones"). Ask, *What*

does it mean to have a cheerful heart? If no one else mentions it, suggest that someone with a cheerful heart is always ready to laugh, even at himself or herself, as long as the humor isn't hurtful or inappropriate.

What happens when you hang around with someone who has a cheerful heart? Suggest that a cheerful heart is contagious. If you're feeling low or struggling in some way, sometimes the best thing you can do for yourself is to spend time with a cheerful person.

Why is it important for Christians to have a cheerful heart? If no one else mentions it, point out that not only do we have a lot to be cheerful about, we also have an opportunity to witness to others through our spirit and attitude. When people see our joy and cheerfulness, they may be inspired to investigate the Source of our joy for themselves.

Pray together, thanking God for giving us so much to be cheerful about. Ask Him to work through your joy and cheerfulness to make Himself known to people who don't yet know Him.

LANGUAGE OF THE DAY

Here's a great way to continue the theme of photos for someone in your family whose primary love language is Receiving Gifts. Create a photo collage that includes some of the person's favorite people, favorite activities, and favorite places. Personalize in a way that says, "I know you, and I want to celebrate the things you love." Hang the collage in his or her room as a surprise.

TO NEXT ADVENTURE

A GRAND WELCOME

WELCOME BACK!

Make plans to greet someone at the airport—
or just to spend part of the day there.

24

GETTING READY

There are two ways to approach this adventure. The
first is to plan a surprise greeting for a friend or loved
one who is returning from a trip. In that case, you'll
need the person's travel itinerary. You'll also need to
check the flight information periodically to make sure
the plane isn't delayed. Plan to arrive at the airport
shortly before the plane's arrival. Allow enough time to
park and get to the meeting point. If spectacle is your
thing, prepare some signs and balloons for the occasion.

ADVENTURE TIME

If your airport adventure involves greeting a friend or
a loved one, make your presence known. React with a

generous amount of excitement when you see the person. Let everyone in the vicinity know just how excited you are to be reunited again. If you can surprise or embarrass your friend or loved one in the process, so much the better.

The second approach to this adventure is simply to watch people at the airport. If that's the option you choose, you might want to add an element of competition by turning it into a scavenger hunt. Hand out a list of things to look for and have your family members check them off when they find them. (If they have their own phones or devices, you might require them to offer photographic proof of their finds.) Your list might include . . .

- ▶ a person wearing a Hawaiian shirt

- ▶ a person wearing a cowboy hat

- ▶ another family waiting for someone to arrive

- ▶ a person who is not dressed for the weather

- ▶ a person wearing a Chicago Cubs baseball cap

Talk about the people you saw while you enjoy a meal together at the airport food court.

THAT REMINDS ME

Share some of your most memorable airport horror stories—the time you got snowed in at O'Hare or missed your connecting flight at LaGuardia. Or perhaps you've had some interesting experiences with the TSA. Keep the tone light and humorous as you share your stories. Talk about any unexpected graces you experienced in the midst of your woes—perhaps a generous fellow passenger or an airline representative who went above and beyond the call of duty for you.

Remind your family members that a lot of good things happen at airports, too. People reunite with loved ones. They begin exciting vacations. They celebrate being home after a long business trip. They buy things duty-free.

FAMILY DEVOTIONS

Suggest that the happy reunions and the sad goodbyes you see at the airport are part of God's plan. Have someone read Genesis 2:18 ("The LORD God said, 'It is not good for the man to be alone. I will make a helper suitable for him'"). Ask, *How do you feel when you're alone or away from the people you love?* If no one else mentions it, point out that while everyone enjoys some alone time, being away from loved ones for too long makes us lonely. That's because we're not experiencing the connections that God created us to enjoy. It's like a part of us is missing. When we reconnect, we feel whole again.

Have someone read 1 Corinthians 1:4 ("I always thank my God for you because of his grace given you in Christ Jesus") and 1 Peter 5:14 ("Greet one another with a kiss of love. Peace to all of you who are in Christ").

Say something like this: *We can't always prevent being separated from our loved ones. That's part of life. What we can do, though, is enjoy one another's company when we are together.*

That's what the apostle Paul was talking about—celebrating the connections God gave us. That goes for our immediate family, our church family, and all of our loved ones.

LANGUAGE OF THE DAY

If you're at the airport with someone whose primary love language is Receiving Gifts, you can create a lasting memory of your adventure by stopping at a duty-free store before you leave. Find just the right present to serve as a memento of the day.

TO NEXT ADVENTURE

ADOPT A GRANDPARENT

Make a new friend from the Greatest Generation.

25

GETTING READY

If you personally don't know of an elderly person who would welcome periodic visits with your family, talk to your pastor or your circle of acquaintances. If that doesn't work, talk to the director of a local retirement home. Explain what you want to do—establish a friendship with someone who would enjoy your family's company—and see if you can get recommendations.

ADVENTURE TIME

Your primary goal with this adventure is to spend time with someone who would like some company. The way you spend your time will depend largely on the particular circumstances you encounter. If your new friend is mobile, you may want to meet for dinner at a restaurant or at your house. (Unless the person insists, you don't want him or her to feel obligated to host your family.)

If your friend is in a care facility, make arrangements to spend time in a semi-private area where everyone can be comfortable as you settle in to get to know one another. You might

want to come armed with a jigsaw puzzle, board game, or playing cards, if you think an icebreaker might help set the mood.

You'll also want to prepare some questions ahead of time to fuel your conversation. Get to know your new friend to the extent that he or she is comfortable sharing. Where

was he born? In how many different places has she lived? What did he do for a living? What are some of her favorite memories? What hobbies does he enjoy? What kind of books does she like to read? Your goal is to find common ground that you can build a relationship on.

Help your family understand that this adventure is more than just a half-day excursion. Ideally you'll be laying the groundwork for an ongoing relationship—one that will require continuing time and effort from your family. Ask each of your family members to commit to this new friendship.

THAT REMINDS ME

On your way home from your visit, talk about your own grandparents—or other relatives or perhaps neighbors whom you watched grow old. Share your memories of them when they were younger and talk about the events and circumstances that made you aware of their mortality. For some people, it's a fall—a broken hip or some other debilitating injury that begins a physical decline. For others, it's the early signs of dementia or Alzheimer's. For others, it's the loss of a spouse.

Point out that everyone who lives to be a certain age will experience the challenges that come with getting older. Suggest that when it comes to interacting with elderly people, there are two good rules of thumb. The first is the Golden Rule: treat them the way you want to be treated when you're old—that is, with dignity, respect, and loving concern. The second is the example of Jesus. We should have the same heart for the elderly that the Lord has.

FAMILY DEVOTIONS

Have someone read Psalm 68:5 ("A father to the fatherless, a defender of widows, is God in his holy dwelling") and Luke 7:11–17, in which Jesus resurrects the son of a widow. Say something like this: *The Lord has a special place in His heart for people who have no one to care for them. And if our goal is to be like Him, we need to make a special place in our hearts for them, as well.*

Have someone read James 1:27 ("Religion that God our Father accepts as pure and faultless is this: to look after orphans and widows in their distress and to keep oneself from being polluted by the world").

Ask, *What are some specific things we can do to "look after" our new friend in a way that pleases the Lord? How can we share God's love with them?* Encourage your family members to offer several ideas, including ways to be a witness of your faith, which you can use in your next visit.

LANGUAGE OF THE DAY

If Words of Affirmation is the primary love language of someone in your family, make note of how that person interacts with your family's adopted grandparent. After your adventure, pull the person aside and share the good things you observed. Help your loved one understand exactly what he or she has to offer your elderly friend.

TO NEXT ADVENTURE

FAMILY VS. FAMILY

Challenge another family to an afternoon of silly competitions.

26

GETTING READY

The key to success in this adventure is finding the right family to join you in it. The ideal candidates will be similar in age and family size to yours. Most importantly, they will have a healthy sense of fun and competition—in that order. If the games become too competitive, you'll lose the spirit of what you're trying to do. Set the tone for the day by being a gracious loser—and an even more gracious winner.

ADVENTURE TIME

Plan a series of contests that don't necessarily require athletic skill—games that realistically can be won by any contestant, regardless of age or ability. For example, your competitions might include

- ► target shooting with rubber bands

- ► a tricycle race (using timed heats, so that each person is racing only the clock)

- ► an obstacle course that must be crawled (again with contestants racing the clock)

- ► tower building, using Jenga blocks

- ► a relay race in which contestants place a balloon between their knees, walk to a chair, place the balloon on the seat, pop it by sitting on it, and then run back to tag the next person.

Come up with some contests of your own and invite your guests to do the same.

Depending on how elaborate you want to get, you might consider awarding gold, silver, and bronze medals (the plastic kind, which can be purchased inexpensively in bulk) to the top three finishers in each event.

THAT REMINDS ME

Use the activity to springboard into a discussion about competitiveness. Talk about who you felt competitive with when you were younger and why. Remind your family members that competitiveness doesn't always involve measurable things like sports and school grades. Sometimes two people compete for the same girl or guy. Sometimes siblings compete for the affection of their parents.

Let that lead into a discussion of healthy competition and unhealthy competition. Ask your family members to offer examples of both. If no one else mentions it, make the point that if a competitive situation causes us to cheat or sacrifice our integrity in other ways—or if it leaves us feeling insecure or doubting our worth—it's unhealthy. By the same token, competition that inspires us to do our best or pushes us to the limits of our ability is healthy.

FAMILY DEVOTIONS

Have someone read Proverbs 27:17 ("As iron sharpens iron, so one person sharpens another"). Ask, *How does iron sharpen iron?* If no one else mentions it, point out that knives are sharpened by being ground against a hard, rough surface—something that can stand up to the strength of the blade. There's nothing smooth or easy about the process. In fact, sparks usually fly when iron sharpens iron.

Ask, *How do people sharpen one another?* If no one else mentions it, suggest that our interactions with others can make us sharper and better people. Sometimes that occurs in competitive situations, when other people push us to do our best. Sometimes that occurs during confrontations, when other people challenge or force us to reconsider our beliefs and opinions. This sharpening also occurs in the church. The members of Christ's body have been brought together to encourage one another to grow more like Christ. There's nothing smooth or easy about that process either. Sometimes different kinds of sparks fly when other people sharpen us. But if we surround ourselves with people of integrity, wisdom, and spiritual maturity, we can take comfort in the fact that God is using them to sharpen us for His purposes.

Offer an example of how you were "sharpened" by someone else. What were the circumstances? What did the person say or do? How did you react? How did the interaction change you? How do you feel about it today? Give your family members a concrete example of what sharpening looks like.

LANGUAGE OF THE DAY

If Physical Touch is the primary love language of someone in your family, find opportunities throughout your competition to accommodate him or her. Work up a multistep handshake or fist bump you can do before each contest. Offer congratulatory hugs and high fives afterward.

TO NEXT ADVENTURE

TOILET PAPER OLYMPICS

Plan a series of contests that involve
toilet paper or toilet paper rolls.

27

GETTING READY

To prepare, you can start hoarding toilet paper and
saving empty toilet paper tubes. The more rolls
and tubes you have to work with, the more options
you'll have when it comes to games and activities.

Hype your event by posting signs, written on
toilet paper, that announce, "Coming Soon: Toilet
Paper Olympics!" or "All Hail the Toilet Paper
Olympians!" If you want to show how serious you
really are about the Olympiad, let your family
members catch you curling toilet paper rolls or doing
some kind of other theme-appropriate training.

ADVENTURE TIME

The rule is simple: if it involves toilet paper or toilet paper rolls and can be turned into a contest that's fair for everyone in your family, it can be included in the Toilet Paper Olympics.

▸ **Speed Mummying** – Contestants will compete in pairs or teams. The goal is to wrap one team member from head to toe with toilet paper. The first team to completely cover its player, so that no trace of the person is visible, wins.

▸ **Toilet Paper Roll Bowling** – Contestants will use a tennis ball to try to knock down empty toilet paper rolls. The standard rules and scoring of bowling apply.

▸ **Monument Building** – Contestants will compete to see who can build the tallest monument, using toilet paper rolls, in five minutes. You may need a chair or step stool for smaller contestants.

▸ **Unbroken** – Contestants will compete to see who can unroll the longest unbroken stream of toilet paper with one toss.

▸ **Plunger Challenge** – Contestants will compete in a timed event in which they run to a stack of toilet paper rolls, use a (brand-new, straight from the package, never-been-used) toilet plunger to pick up a roll, transport it back to the start-finish line and then repeat the process until all rolls have been collected. Contestants may use only the plunger to pick up the rolls.

Customize your Toilet Paper Olympics by adding your own events or tweaking the rules of these events to better fit your family.

THAT REMINDS ME

Obviously this activity lends itself to reminiscing about "TP-ing" as a kid. If you have a story about being the perpetrator or victim of a "TP" attack, share it. If possible, share your memories of the aftermath. If you were the perpetrator, did you get caught? If so, what happened? If you were the victim, did you have to clean it up? How did your parents react?

Let that lead into a discussion about decision-making. Point out that there are certain decisions we make that may not be the best, but aren't necessarily harmful—as long as we're willing to face the consequences. TP-ing someone's house is a good example of this. There are other decisions, however, that *are* harmful—even if we don't recognize it at the time. Smoking your first cigarette or drinking your first alcohol may seem harmless in the moment, but may lead to a lifetime of addiction. Saying something cruel to someone for a laugh may seem harmless in the moment, but may affect that person's self-esteem for years. Emphasize the importance of using wise judgment in making decisions both big and small.

FAMILY DEVOTIONS

Say something like this: *Today we had fun using toilet paper in ways that it wasn't meant to be used. But if we did this every day, we would be wasting something valuable—something that is made for a specific and very useful purpose. That same principle applies to our lives.*

Read Ephesians 1:11 ("In him we were also chosen, having been predestined according to the plan of him who works out everything in conformity with the purpose of his will"). Point out that God made each of your family members for a specific purpose: to use the gifts and abilities He has given each of them to bring glory to Him.

Ask, *What kind of gifts and abilities has He given us?* Be prepared to name at least one or two specific gifts for each family member. Point out that there are many skills and abilities your family members have yet to discover.

Ask, *How can you use those gifts and abilities to bring glory to God?* Encourage each of your group members to offer an idea or two. Point out that even though it may seem fun to do things that aren't necessarily in line with our God-given purpose, ultimately we're most valuable doing what we were made to do.

LANGUAGE OF THE DAY

You can make the day of a family member whose primary love language is Quality Time by pairing with him or her during every team activity—and perhaps taking some toilet-paper-themed selfies together along the way.

TO NEXT ADVENTURE

EVERY DAY IS A HOLIDAY

28

Choose an obscure holiday to celebrate
as you would a major holiday.

GETTING READY

Conduct an online search for obscure holidays.
You'll find everything from National Spaghetti Day
(January 4) to National Goof Off Day (March 22)
to National Cheeseburger Day (September 18).
Find one that you think will fit your purposes.
Decorate your house accordingly.

ADVENTURE TIME

Obviously your adventure will depend on the
holiday you choose. For example, if you choose
National Bird Day (January 5), you might visit the
bird section of your local zoo or go bird-watching at
a local park. You might check out from the library a

field guide to birds in your area. You might watch a movie that features birds, such as the animated film *Rio*. You might build and decorate a birdhouse. You might avoid chicken or turkey for your meals.

If you choose National Astronomy Day (October 5), you might visit a planetarium or space museum. You might create models of the planets in our solar system using Styrofoam balls and paint or markers. You might borrow a telescope so that your family can do its own investigation of the stars. You might watch a movie that involves space exploration. You might serve Tang, the beverage of astronauts, with a meal.

If you really want to get into the spirit of the holiday, make greeting cards in the best Hallmark tradition and deliver them to neighbors, grandparents, and friends. Act surprised when they admit that they didn't realize it was National Bird or Astronomy Day.

THAT REMINDS ME

Talk about special days your family celebrated when you were growing up—events and commemorations that were meaningful to you, but perhaps not as meaningful to other families. If, say, your family takes pride in its Norwegian or Hispanic heritage, you may celebrate certain holidays that aren't on American calendars.

Or if there's an annual event that looms large in your state or area—the Indianapolis 500 or Kentucky Derby, for example—your family may have built traditions around it.

Lead into a discussion of holidays you would like to celebrate or days that you think should be declared holidays. Talk about why we celebrate certain days and ignore others. If the conversation continues to flow, you might ask for suggestions for brand-new holidays. Encourage each person to make up a holiday, set a date for when it should be observed, and offer some ideas about how to celebrate it.

FAMILY DEVOTIONS

Say something like this: *Even if we didn't have a calendar that listed every goofy holiday ever created, we would still have reason to treat every day like it's special.* Have someone read Psalm 118:24 ("This is the day that the LORD has made; let us rejoice and be glad in it," ESV).

Ask, *How is today different from yesterday?* If no one else mentions it, point out that it's different in *every* way. Every sunrise brings with it a do-over. No matter what happened yesterday, today offers a fresh start—new blessings, new opportunities, new encounters, new experiences.

Ask, *How can we rejoice and be glad for this day that God has given us?* If no one else mentions it, suggest that you can pray—and then do just that. Praise God for His gift of a new day. Ask Him to give you the wisdom and courage to wring every bit of blessing from it.

LANGUAGE OF THE DAY

Certain "holidays"—such as "Make Your Dream Come True Day" (January 13)—lend themselves to focus on one person. If Acts of Service is the primary love language of someone in your family, build your day around that person. (If that person is your only child, this will be easier to do.) Plan a day that celebrates their favorite things and includes their favorite activities and meals.

TO NEXT ADVENTURE

INVENTION EXCHANGE

Let your imaginations soar as you brainstorm and present ideas for new inventions.

29

GETTING READY

Show your family pictures or videos of famous inventors and their inventions. Do a little research to get an idea of how their ideas came to them, how many times they failed before they came up with something that worked and how they benefited (or failed to benefit) from their invention. You can start with inventors such as Thomas Edison, Nikola Tesla, Alexander Graham Bell, and Eli Whitney.

ADVENTURE TIME

Give your family free rein in imagining new and wondrous creations. Don't worry about nagging problems such as the laws of physics or the limits of current technology. Encourage your family members to dream up anything they think would make life better, easier, faster, or more fun.

Present the inventions to one another, using pictures, descriptions, or prototypes, depending on how much time you have. Give each person time to explain what their invention is called, what it does, who will be able to use it, and how it will change the world or make life better for people.

You could take things a step further and have your inventors talk about how they would market their creations—specifically, what kind of commercials they would use to make people interested in it—and how much they would charge for it.

THAT REMINDS ME

Spend some time talking about how technology has changed since you were your kids' age. The obvious place to start is with phone technology, especially if you grew up when cellphones were used only for calls. Talk about the many things that have become almost obsolete, thanks to new inventions and new technology. The list would include everything from folded car maps that you keep in your glove compartment to CD players.

Lead into a discussion of how technology likely will be different when your kids are your age. What will phones and personal devices look like? What will they be able to do? Will people still drive cars? Will tourists be able to visit the moon? Talk about which of your inventions is most likely to exist twenty-five years from now.

FAMILY DEVOTIONS

Have someone read Exodus 31:1–5 and 2 Chronicles 2:5–7. Point out that innovation has been around forever, even in biblical times. But there are two ways to approach innovation and the human quest to push boundaries and discover new frontiers. The first is found in Genesis 11, where the people tried to build a tower that reached heaven. Because their motivation was selfish and evil, God stopped them.

The other approach is found in 1 Corinthians 10:31 ("So whether you eat or drink or whatever you do, do it all for the glory of God"). The word *whatever* includes inventions and technology. As long as we're trying to bring glory to God, He will bless what we do.

Ask, *How do you know if something is bringing glory to God?* If no one else mentions it, suggest that it comes down to what it's used for and who gets the credit for it. When the astronauts of Apollo 8 were orbiting the moon and transmitting a broadcast back to Earth, they decided to read the story of creation from Genesis. All of their cutting-edge space technology had caused them to look in awe at their Creator, who made it possible.

LANGUAGE OF THE DAY

You can do something special for a son or daughter whose primary love language is Acts of Service. For your invention, brainstorm an idea that would specifically benefit this family member. For example, if he or she enjoys marching band, you might come up with a virtual-reality program that projects virtual band members doing a routine, which would allow your family member to practice at home.

TO NEXT ADVENTURE

OBSTACLE COURSE

Create an obstacle course in your backyard.

30

GETTING READY

Raid your attic, basement, and garage for items that can be used in an obstacle course. Use them in conjunction with the natural features of your yard (hills and trees), as well as the man-made structures (swing sets, trailers, and sheds), to create a course that is long and involved. If your yard is small, establish a route that circles your house three or four times, with each lap incorporating different obstacles.

Your goal is to create a course that is challenging the first time you run it and then a little less so each subsequent time. Make sure you have an accurate stopwatch and a log to record times.

ADVENTURE TIME

Let your imaginations run wild as you create your course. It's okay to scatter in a few "traditional" obstacles, such as a pylon slalom course, but make sure the bulk of your obstacles are nontraditional. For example, if you have a spare length of rope, you might create an obstacle that requires contestants to lasso a fencepost before they continue on.

Make sure that your course has plenty of "equalizers," obstacles that favor younger, smaller contestants. A limbo pole would be an effective equalizer, as would a narrow tunnel or a pogo stick. You also want to make sure that no obstacle is too difficult for someone in your family to complete. Your goal is

to create a challenging course, not one that frustrates people.

If your family is competitive, you could set up some official rules. For example, you might limit each person to two "official" qualifying heats, in which each lap is carefully timed. All other runs will be considered unofficial practice attempts. The qualifying times will then determine the order in which everyone runs the final timed heat. The person with the fastest time in the final heat is declared the champion. (You can find inexpensive plastic trophies and medals at any party store, if you would like to hand out awards afterward.)

Once you've gotten your course just right, and you've had a chance to compete on it with your family, invite kids in the neighborhood to try it out.

THAT REMINDS ME

After you've gone through the course several times, shift your focus from physical obstacles to personal obstacles. Talk about some of the obstacles you've faced in your life. Start out with some light-hearted ones. Perhaps you had a fear of the dark when you were a kid or you had trouble learning to ride a bike. Work your way up to more serious obstacles. Perhaps a learning disability presented challenges in school. Perhaps a lack of self-confidence kept you from dating. Talk openly (and age-appropriately) about how those obstacles affected you.

Discuss the strategies you used for dealing with the obstacles and ultimately overcoming them. Talk about the impact the experience of overcoming your obstacles had on you. Did it give you a sense of pride? Did it make you more aware of the obstacles that other people face? Did it give you confidence?

FAMILY DEVOTIONS

Say something like this: *God's Word has something to say about obstacles and difficult situations.*

Have someone read James 1:2–4 ("Consider it pure joy, my brothers and sisters, whenever you face trials of many kinds, because you know that the testing of your faith produces perseverance. Let perseverance finish its work so that you may be mature and complete, not lacking anything"). Ask, *What do obstacles do for us?* If no one else mentions it, point out that they make us stronger spiritually. Every time we overcome an obstacle, we gain wisdom and confidence. We become better prepared to face obstacles in the future.

What should be our first step when we face an obstacle in our lives? If no one else mentions it, suggest that praying is always the best strategy.

Pray together, thanking God for walking beside us when we face obstacles. Ask Him to help your family members maintain a proper perspective when obstacles arise.

LANGUAGE OF THE DAY

If Quality Time is the primary love language of one of your family members, you can incorporate quality time into your course-building. Team up with them to create a special obstacle together. Brainstorm ideas with him or her and then spend some uninterrupted time together building, positioning, and testing the obstacle together.

TO NEXT ADVENTURE

SOMETHING NEW

Plan an adventure filled with new
things and new experiences.

31

GETTING READY

Do a little investigating. Are there any new restaurants
in your area? Any new parks or places to explore?
Any new stores that would be of interest to your
family? Any new movies opening at the multiplex?
If so, consider how you might work them into your
adventure.

For maximum effect, try scheduling this adventure on the first day of a new week, the first day of
a new month, the first day of a new season, or the
first day of a new year.

ADVENTURE TIME

"New" can be worked into a variety of activities.
For example, you could go out for doughnuts or ice

cream and make a rule that everyone has to order a new flavor, one that they've never had before. The meals you serve could be made up of new dishes, ones you've never served before.

If you take a walk as a family, you could search out a new route, one you've never taken before. If you play a board game or card game, make it one that none of you has ever played before. If your kids are young enough for bedtime stories, bring home some new children's books from the library.

You can take this idea as far as you'd like. For example, you may coordinate your adventure with back-to-school shopping and have everyone dress in new clothes. Or you may coordinate it with haircut day so that everyone has a new hairstyle. Whatever you do, make it a day of firsts for your family.

THAT REMINDS ME

Talk about how you felt about new things when you were a kid. Were you an adventurous eater, always eager to try new foods? Were you the first in line when new movies came out? Did you insist on wearing new clothes as often as possible? Did you drive a new car? Compare your own attitude toward new things with that of your kids.

Talk about why new things seem so appealing—and why some people are willing to pay so much for them. Ask your family members to weigh in on how long it takes for new things to lose their luster.

FAMILY DEVOTIONS

Suggest that *new* is one of the best words in the Bible. Have someone read 2 Corinthians 5:17 ("Therefore, if anyone is in

Christ, the new creation has come: The old has gone, the new is here!"). Explain that sin can make us feel dirty and worthless. But Jesus makes us new. He gives us a fresh start. We no longer have to feel guilty about the things we've done.

Have someone read Lamentations 3:22–23 ("Because of the LORD's great love we are not consumed, for his compassions never fail. They are new every morning; great is your faithfulness"). Point out to your family members that every day has the potential to be incredible, to show or teach us something new. Every day gives us a chance to get a fresh perspective on an old problem. No matter how bad today has been, tomorrow has the potential to be better because it's new.

Pray together, thanking God for the new blessings He gives us every day. Ask Him to give your family members the wisdom to understand that no matter how bad a particular day is, the next day brings a fresh start.

LANGUAGE OF THE DAY

If Receiving Gifts is the primary love language of someone in your family, you can do something meaningful for them in conjunction with this adventure. If they collect something, whether it's action figures, snow globes, or something else, give him or her something *new* to add to the collection.

TO NEXT ADVENTURE

SOMETHING BORROWED

32 Spend a day doing activities suggested by other people, using things that they supply you with.

GETTING READY

The best way to prepare for this adventure is to put out the word to your friends, family members, and coworkers that you're looking for activities you can do with your family. Ask them to tell you about their favorite things to do with their families. If one or more of their ideas seems good, pursue it. And if one or more of their ideas requires special equipment, ask to borrow theirs.

The right people to approach are those who are passionate about their hobbies and pastimes—and who are eager to introduce them to others. If you have a few people in your circle of acquaintances who fit that bill, you can plan a memorable adventure with your family.

ADVENTURE TIME

Sometimes the best adventures are new adventures, so seek out ideas for activities that are new to your family. On a grand scale, that might involve borrowing a tent and camping equipment and heading to a friend's favorite camping spot. On a smaller scale, that might involve borrowing anything from a bocce ball set to board games you've never played to movies you've never watched—all on the recommendation of others.

You can take the idea as far as you like—or as far as your friends and family are willing to play along. Some people may be willing to give recommendations for a new restaurant you should try. Others may be willing to lend you their car, their boat, or perhaps even their clothes, if you really want to take it to the next level.

THAT REMINDS ME

Point out that borrowing doesn't always involve possessions. People borrow clothing styles, ways of talking (expressions), ways of thinking, and many other things from other people—sometimes without even realizing it. Share some of the ways you've been influenced in a positive way by others. Talk about why those people had such a good impact on you.

Lead into a discussion of influences that aren't so good. If you have some relevant examples from your own life, share them. Talk about why you allowed yourself to be influenced in a negative way or why you "borrowed" certain bad habits from others. Spend some time talking about how you can tell whether someone is a good influence or a bad influence. If no one else mentions it, suggest that sometimes you have to rely on loved ones—people who have your best interests at heart—to tell you when they think you're being influenced in a negative way.

FAMILY DEVOTIONS

Ask, *What do you think the Bible says about lending and borrowing?* Have your family members take turns reading Psalm 37:21 ("The wicked borrow and do not repay, but the righteous give generously"); Proverbs 22:7 ("the borrower is slave to the lender"); Matthew 5:42 ("Give to the one who asks you, and do not turn away from the one who wants to borrow from you"); and Romans 13:8 ("Let no debt remain outstanding").

Ask, *How would you sum up these verses in one or two sentences?* You might suggest something like, *We should give freely yet wisely to those who ask something from us. When we ask something from someone else, we must be diligent about returning it.*

Drive home your point by returning everything you borrowed. Make sure that everything is cleaned and intact, just the way it was when you borrowed it. Offer a heartfelt thank you to those who loaned you the equipment for your adventure. Share your experiences with them. You might also offer a small token of appreciation—perhaps a plate of fresh-baked cookies—to those who generously gave what they had.

LANGUAGE OF THE DAY

You can use the theme of this adventure to do something nice for a family member whose primary love language is Words of Affirmation. Share with that person something intangible you would love to borrow from them, whether it's a kind spirit, a sense of humor, skills in math, or something else. Give the person something to feel proud of.

TO NEXT ADVENTURE

MAKE UP YOUR OWN HOLIDAY

Create a special day, just for the sake of celebrating something with your family.

33

GETTING READY

This adventure expands on a discussion found in the "That Reminds Me" section of the "Every Day Is a Holiday" adventure (page 120). Your preparation will depend on the holiday you create. One option is to buy generic party supplies and decorate them to fit the theme of your holiday.

ADVENTURE TIME

Your first step, obviously, is to choose or create a day to celebrate. You can go in several different directions here. You could do something spiritual, such as "Obscure Bible Story Day." You could do something commemorative, such as celebrating the lives of loved ones who have passed away, and call it "Miss You Day." You could do something obscure, such as "Forgotten Letter Day," in which you celebrate things that begin with "Q," "X," and "Z." You could do something generic, such as "Laughter Day," where you watch your favorite comedy movie, play a game like Charades that inspires laughter, dress up in goofy clothes and wear fake mustaches, and do any other humorous thing you can think of.

Once you've established what it is you want to celebrate, brainstorm "customs and traditions" for your special day. If, for example, you choose to do "Miss You Day," you might establish a tradition of watching old family movies and serving dishes that were specialties or favorites of your deceased loved ones. If you decide to celebrate something more arbitrary and less serious, you might establish a tradition of wearing stripes and talking in whispers. Just keep in mind that whatever you come up with will be in effect for the entire day, so choose your customs and traditions wisely.

If you hit on something your family *really* enjoys with this adventure, do it again. Schedule it for the same day next year, and see if you can start an annual tradition. Who knows? You may come up with the next Festivus.

THAT REMINDS ME

Talk about why people celebrate holidays. It might be interesting to go through the calendar and talk about how some of the major holidays came to be holidays. (The information is easily accessible online.) Talk about why your family celebrates certain holidays, but not others.

FAMILY DEVOTIONS

Say something like this: *Sometimes it's fun to have a day that's different from others. Sometimes a little variety and unpredictability can make things exciting. But not always.*

Have someone read Hebrews 13:8 ("Jesus Christ is the same yesterday and today and forever"). Ask, *In what ways is Jesus always the same?* If no one else mentions it, point out that He isn't controlled by emotions or feelings. He doesn't treat people differently one day from the next. He doesn't change His mind.

Why is it important to know that Jesus never changes? If no one else mentions it, point out that because He never changes, His promises can be trusted. His love for us never changes. Human relationships change all the time. People come and go in our lives. They can leave us feeling unstable and insecure. But in Jesus we have someone who loves us completely—and who always will. We can be secure in His love.

Pray together, praising God for His unchanging nature. Ask Him to give your family members the wisdom to turn to Him when things seem uncertain and unpredictable.

 ## LANGUAGE OF THE DAY

If Quality Time is the primary love language of one of your family members, make sure that at least part of your special day includes an interest that the two of you share. For example, if you were to celebrate "Laughter Day," you could make sure that part of your celebration involves watching a cartoon or TV show that makes the two of you laugh.

TO NEXT ADVENTURE

MAKEOVERS

34

Everyone takes a turn in the makeup chair for a new look.

GETTING READY

Preparation is essential for this adventure, especially when it comes to "serious" makeovers. You'll need to consider *how* to make over each person in your family. Spend some time studying potential hairstyles and new ways of doing makeup. If you want to invest some money in the adventure, buy new clothes for each person—ones that are a departure from the person's usual outfits. (Consignment stores offer stylish clothes at discounted prices.)

For crazy makeovers, make sure you have a variety of hair-coloring sprays and face paints. Look for online tutorials on how to create animal faces or ghoulish looks.

ADVENTURE TIME

How drastically can your family change one another's appearance? That question lies at the heart of this adventure. Each person will get to choose whether to submit to a serious makeover or a crazy one.

A serious makeover will involve a new hairstyle, a new way of doing makeup, a new outfit (one that's different from the person's normal style)—or some combination thereof. Make sure you have plenty of sculpting gel, hairspray, curling irons, and flat irons to go around. Put some thought into these makeovers. Give your family members some new style ideas to consider.

A crazy makeover will involve a (temporary) change of hair color; funny, scary, or weird face paintings; and maybe a few temporary tattoos, for good measure. It's your choice as to whether you let each person have a say in their crazy makeover or whether they must wait until a "big reveal" to discover what you've done.

Of course, what's good for the goose is good for the gander. In addition to supervising your family's makeovers, you have to be willing to submit to one of your own. Your attitude will go a long way toward setting the tone for the adventure, so be a good sport.

THAT REMINDS ME

Talk about how your personal style has evolved over the years. Was there a time when you were younger that you spent hours on your hair, face, clothes, and other aspects of your appearance? Has that changed? If so, in what way? How do you explain the change? Or is the reverse true? Were you less interested in your appearance when you were younger than you are now? If you have some of your old school pictures handy, put them on display to offer some visual evidence of your evolving style.

Talk about the reasons we put time and effort into looking our best. Do we do it to feel good about ourselves? Do we do it for the approval of others? Let that lead into a discussion of how we know when we're focusing too much—or too little—on our outward appearance. You might also talk about how other people's opinions should and shouldn't influence us.

FAMILY DEVOTIONS

Say something like this: *Looks can be deceiving. Some people who appear to be flawless and put together on the outside may be struggling terribly on the inside. And some of the most genuinely beautiful people in the world will never appear in a magazine or a runway because their beauty is inside. The Old Testament offers a great example of this.*

Explain that when the people of Israel got to the land that God had promised them, they asked God for a king, like other nations had. God gave them Saul, who was tall and striking—someone who *looked* like a king. But looks can be deceiving; Saul was a bad king. So God sent His prophet Samuel to find the next king—one who would become the greatest, besides Jesus, in Israel's history. God told Samuel that he would find this new king in the house of Jesse.

Have your family members take turns reading 1 Samuel 16:4–13. Ask, *Why did Samuel assume that Eliab was the one God had chosen?* If no one else mentions it, point out that

Samuel was judging by status and outward appearance. Eliab was Jesse's oldest son, tall and handsome. But He wasn't the one God had chosen.

Ask, *What happens if we consider people's appearance too much today?* If no one else mentions it, suggest that we would never get to know what's inside the person—the things that *really* matter.

LANGUAGE OF THE DAY

If Words of Affirmation is the primary love language of someone in your family, build him or her up with sincere compliments and observations while you do your makeover. Identify various attractive qualities—both inner and outer—that you see. Make sure they know that the makeover is just a change of pace, and not an effort to make him or her look "better."

TO NEXT ADVENTURE

35

Why should the spirit of Christmas be confined to a single season?

GETTING READY

If you're going to shop for Christmas gifts, it helps to have a list. Before you go out, ask your family members to write down two or three things they would like for Christmas. You may or may not want to set a price range for the items people put on their list.

You may also want to coordinate your adventure with the retail calendar. Many retailers offer "Christmas in July" sales. Not only will you get better deals, you may also get to enjoy some out-of-season seasonal decorations.

ADVENTURE TIME

The buying is secondary in this adventure. Your primary goal is to have fun with your family, defying the calendar and celebrating the Christmas season months before the real thing. Choose the way you want to celebrate. If that involves wearing ugly Christmas sweaters or a Santa's cap while you shop, so be it. If it involves putting up lights and tinsel around your house, so be it.

Make a playlist of your favorite Christmas songs to listen to in the car. And, speaking of music, if you know of friends or family members who would appreciate the gesture, you might do a little caroling in front of their houses.

Swing by your local library on your way home and pick up some Christmas-themed children's books—and perhaps a DVD copy of *A Christmas Story*, *A Christmas Carol*, *How the Grinch Stole Christmas*, or any of your other holiday favorites.

THAT REMINDS ME

Point out that the true meaning of Christmas— "the reason for the season"—often gets lost in the busyness of December. Talk about the things that demand your family's time in the weeks between Thanksgiving and Christmas. Many high school and college students have final exams during that time. Add to that the pressures of holiday baking, shopping, and entertaining, and it's easy to see how the events of Luke 2 get lost in the shuffle.

Brainstorm some ideas as a family to make this Christmas season different. Think about tweaks you can make to your schedule and priorities you can establish to make sure that

Jesus' birth—and what it means to the world—is the main focus of your Christmas this year.

FAMILY DEVOTIONS

Have your family members take turns reading Luke 2:1–20. Focus your attention on aspects of the Advent that are often overlooked. Explain that Old Testament prophets predicted the details of Jesus' birth hundreds of years before it happened. One of those predictions, found in Micah 5:2, said that He would be born in Bethlehem. That presented a challenge, because Joseph and Mary lived in Nazareth, which was a considerable journey from Bethlehem.

So how did Jesus come to be born in Bethlehem? As Luke explains in his gospel, Caesar Augustus, the emperor of Rome, wanted to collect taxes from the people in his empire. That

 required all men to register in the city or town where their families had come from. Because Joseph's family had come from Bethlehem, he went there, along with his very pregnant wife.

Say something like this: *This is just one of many, many prophecies that Jesus fulfilled. Why do you think God put so many prophecies in His Word?* If no one else mentions it, suggest that fulfilled prophecies give us reason to trust God's Word.

Ask, *Why do you think God used a Roman emperor's tax decree to help fulfill prophecy?* If no one else mentions it, suggest that He was showing that He can work through any circumstances to bring about His will. He was also showing His people who it was that *really* had ultimate authority over them.

Pray together, thanking God for sending His Son to the world to save us from the punishment we deserve for our sin. Ask Him to help you keep the spirit of Christmas—that is, a spirit of gratitude, peace, and goodwill to all—throughout the year.

LANGUAGE OF THE DAY

This adventure offers a golden opportunity to do something special for a family member whose primary love language is Receiving Gifts. Shop online for a Christmas ornament that reflects one of your loved one's hobbies or interests. Wrap the ornament like a Christmas present. (If you have a potted tree in your home, you could place the present under it.) Encourage your loved one to hang the ornament in their room, as a reminder of your adventure, until you put up your Christmas tree.

TO NEXT ADVENTURE

INDOOR CAMPING

36 "Rough it" in your living room, using a tent and other camping equipment.

GETTING READY

If you don't have a tent that will fit in your living room, see if you can borrow one. Otherwise, you'll need to improvise, using blankets, sheets, and anything else that can be used to create a tentlike sleeping area.

You'll also need campfire foods, such as hot dogs, hamburgers, marshmallows, graham crackers, and chocolate bars. If you have a fireplace, make sure that you have enough logs on hand to last you through the night.

ADVENTURE TIME

Set the ground rules for your indoor camping adventure. Turn off all the lights and declare all electrical appliances and devices off-limits. As campers, you may use only what would be available to you on an outdoor camping trip. Hand out flashlights and battery-operated lanterns.

If you have a fireplace in your living room, put it to use. If you embark on this adventure during the cooler months of the year, turn off the heat in your house and let the fireplace keep you warm while you camp. If you have the proper utensils, use the fireplace for cooking hot dogs on a skewer, roasting marshmallows for s'mores, and popping popcorn. This would be a great opportunity to teach your kids how to start a fire in the fireplace, if they don't know already. (If you don't have a fireplace, keep your house's heat on—but leave the lights out. Use your stove to cook.)

Spend your evening enjoying campfire food, singing your favorite campfire songs, telling ghost stories, and playing games by lantern light or flashlight.

 ## THAT REMINDS ME

Your makeshift campfire would be a great place to share your favorite camping stories. If your kids have been to church camp, scout camp, summer camp, or on some other camping excursion, encourage them to talk about some of their favorite memories. What were their cabins like? What kind of mischief did they get into?

Supplement their stories with some of your own. If you camped with your family when you were a kid, talk about your experiences. Were camping trips something that you looked forward to? If so, why? If not, why not? Where did you go? What did you do? What was the worst weather you ever

experienced? What kind of run-
ins did you have with wildlife or
poison ivy?

If none of you have much
experience with camping (the
outdoor type), talk about whether
it seems like something you would like to do.

FAMILY DEVOTIONS

Have someone read (by flashlight) Numbers 9:17–18 ("Whenever the cloud lifted from above the tent, the Israelites set
out; wherever the cloud settled, the Israelites encamped. At
the LORD's command the Israelites set out, and at his command
they encamped. As long as the cloud stayed over the tabernacle,
they remained in camp"). Explain that this passage is talking
about one of the most famous camping trips in history: the
journey of the Hebrew people from slavery in Egypt to the land
that God had promised them.

Remind your family members of some of the details of
the journey: Moses led the Hebrew people, but got tired of
their constant complaining. Along the way, God fed them by
sending manna (bread from heaven) every morning. He caused
water to flow from rocks when they got thirsty. Their journey
could have been much shorter, but they didn't trust God when
He told them to conquer the people who occupied their promised land. As a result, they had to continue their camping trip
in the wilderness for forty more years.

Say something like this: *The Israelites had no food, no water,
and no idea where they were going. They had to rely on God for
everything. Tell me some things that were good about that arrange-*

ment as well as some things that would have been difficult to deal with. If no one else mentions it, point out that God is more trustworthy than any human guide. He has a history of taking care of His people in miraculous ways. On the other hand, not knowing when your journey would end must have been difficult to deal with.

Pray together, thanking God for the evidence He gives us in His Word that He will take care of us. Ask Him to help your family members trust Him when you face difficult or frightening situations.

LANGUAGE OF THE DAY

If Acts of Service is the primary love language of one of your fellow campers, go out of your way to do thoughtful things for him or her during your indoor camping adventure. That may include preparing their bedroll in the tent, making an extra-chocolatey s'more just for them, or volunteering to teach them how to build a fire or pitch a tent.

TO NEXT ADVENTURE

FUN WITH BLINDFOLDS

37

Enjoy games and challenges that
test your sightless skills.

GETTING READY

The preparation for this adventure is minimal. The
first thing you need to do is find an effective blindfold. If you have time, test out different options
to see which is most effective. The second thing
you need to do is make your playing area as safe
as possible. Eventually somebody's bound to trip
and fall. If you can anticipate that beforehand, you
can remove furniture or items from the room that
might cause injury.

ADVENTURE TIME

Plan a series of challenges and games for your family
members to attempt while wearing a blindfold.

Some should be individual efforts; others should involve a non-blindfolded partner who guides and directs the blindfolded person. Here are a few ideas to get you started.

- Pin the _____ on the _____
  The original blindfold game is an ideal starting point for your adventure. But you don't necessarily *have* to follow tradition. Instead of pinning a tail on a donkey, how about taping a mustache on Grandpa? All you need is a cardboard mustache with tape on the back and a framed headshot of Grandpa.

- What *Is* This?
  Blindfolded contestants have to identify unusual objects using just their hands. Objects may include anything from a square of Jello with halved grapes in it to an unusual stuffed animal.

- Blindfolded Easter Egg Hunt
  A non-blindfolded contestant guides his or her blindfolded partner to plastic Easter eggs that are hidden in plain sight. The goal is to find as many eggs as possible in two minutes.

- Blindfolded Obstacle Course
  A non-blindfolded contestant guides his or her blindfolded partner over, under, around, and through obstacles. The pair with the fastest time is declared the winner.

In the paired activities, make sure your partners take turns being the blindfolded one.

THAT REMINDS ME

Ask each of your family members to name some things that they think they could do blindfolded.

Obviously driving is out of the question, but what about walking? Could your kids walk to school or the local playground or a friend's house blindfolded? Could you walk your dog around the block blindfolded?

Think about chores. Could you make a bed blindfolded? Could you prepare a meal blindfolded? Could you *eat* a meal blindfolded, for that matter? Talk about the likely results of doing certain things blindfolded.

FAMILY DEVOTIONS

Say something like this: *Blindfolded people aren't the only ones who need someone to show them the way. We all do, at some point or another. That's because we all face situations or stages of life that we've never encountered before. So we're not prepared for them. When we face situations like that, it's nice to have someone who* has *experienced them before. Someone who has helpful wisdom and knowledge to pass along to us. Someone who can guide us so that we're not stumbling along blindly.*

Have someone read Proverbs 11:14 ("victory is won through many advisers") and Proverbs 15:22 ("Plans fail for lack of counsel, but with many advisers they succeed"). Ask, *What should we look for in an adviser?* If no one else mentions it, suggest that an adviser should be someone who is spiritually mature, honest, and trustworthy.

How can you find advisers you trust? If no one else mentions it, suggest that you start with people who care about you—

people who want to see you succeed and have your best interests at heart. From there, you ask questions and listen. You weigh the advice you get to determine whether it's sound or not. People who consistently give you sound advice, whether you want to hear it or not, are the ones whose opinions should start to matter to you.

LANGUAGE OF THE DAY

Make sure that at some point during your adventure, you team up with a family member whose primary love language is Quality Time. Savor the one-on-one moments you have together—serving as one another's "eyes" and navigating obstacles as one. Talk about why you make such a great team.

TO NEXT ADVENTURE

BOOK CHALLENGE

38

Enjoy a mini-marathon of reading with your family.

GETTING READY

Your preparation for this adventure is a visit to the library. Spend some time searching for books for your marathon. Select just the right mixture of old favorites, new releases, and other titles that look promising. Ask a librarian for assistance. Briefly explain the adventure you have planned and ask for recommendations. Beyond that, the only thing you need to do is create a reading-friendly environment in your home.

ADVENTURE TIME

This adventure is a quest—a quest to read as many books (if your kids are young enough to enjoy short children's books) or as many pages (if your kids enjoy longer books) as you can in a single afternoon. If you have young children who can't read on their own, you and your spouse can take turns reading aloud to them. You can switch off every hour so that you each have time to read on your own. (If you'd rather focus on reading quality over reading quantity, you can make this adventure a quest to read a book and remember as much of the story as possible. Each family member will read a story that is new to them, then retell it to the family. The winner is whoever does the best job retelling the story and remembers the most details from their particular book.)

Keep track of your book or page totals on a white board. If you want to add an element of excitement to your adventure, keep a "countdown clock" running so that your kids know how much time you have left.

This would be a great rainy day or snow day activity. It's also an adventure that screams for staying in your pajamas all day, perhaps in front of a roaring fire or on a nice dry porch. Ask your family members to give up their phones, devices, and electronic equipment during your reading adventure. Print books are preferable to eBooks for this adventure. There is less temptation to be distracted if you cannot click out of your book and onto the internet.

THAT REMINDS ME

After your marathon has ended, reminisce about the books your parents, or perhaps even your grandparents, used to read to you. Did you have any favorite books? Was there one person you preferred to have read to you? If so, what was it about that person's reading style that made it special for you?

Talk about how your taste in books evolved as you got older. Did you go through a mystery or science fiction phase? Did you make an effort to read the "classics," the books that experts consider to be the greatest ever written? Did you discover any favorite authors along the way?

Share a list of your five favorite books. Explain what each one is about, when you first read it and why it meant (and still means) so much to you. Encourage your family members to share some of their favorite books as well.

FAMILY DEVOTIONS

Say something like this: *A book can entertain us, scare us, make us laugh or cry, make us care about the characters in it, introduce us to a new world, or show us a new way of looking at the world. But there's only one book that reveals God's will and His plan for our lives.*

Remind them that just like they had to pay close attention to the book they read, it is always important to pay the closest attention to the words of the  Bible. We shouldn't read the Bible simply to check a box. As Simon Peter once said to Jesus, "Lord, to whom shall we go? You have the words of eternal life" (John 6:68). The Bible's words are the light that shows us how to live as God's children.

Have someone read Psalm 119:105 ("Your word is a lamp for my feet, a light on my path"). Ask, *In what way is the Bible a lamp for our feet and a light on our path?* If no one else mentions it, point out that God's Word shows us where to go. It gives us instructions on how to live; it warns us what to avoid. Best of all, though, it shows us *who* to follow. Jesus set an example for His followers.

LANGUAGE OF THE DAY

If Physical Touch is the primary love language of one of your children, take advantage of the opportunity to spend an entire afternoon communicating in his or her language. Create a cozy book nook where you can cuddle with your child. Whether you sit or lie next to him or her, make sure that you maintain consistent physical contact while you read.

TO NEXT ADVENTURE

FACE YOUR FEARS

39

Create a family bonding opportunity while you stare down the things that scare you silly.

GETTING READY

Chances are, you're aware of the fears and phobias of your family members. Still, it might be helpful to have a conversation in which everyone feels free to share secret or not-so-secret phobias. You could lead by example by sharing one or more of your own.

Your preparation will depend on the fears your family members identify. If speaking or performing in public is someone's fear, find a family-friendly karaoke restaurant. If someone has a fear of heights, make arrangements to visit a tall building with an observation deck or a natural overlook with a steep drop. If someone has a fear of spiders or snakes, find a petting zoo that offers a chance to interact with them.

ADVENTURE TIME

Your goal in this adventure is to give your family members an *opportunity* to face their fears in a relaxed, nonthreatening atmosphere. If your arachnophobic family member isn't ready to have a spider crawling on his or her arm in a petting zoo, try a realistic-looking rubber one—or just a picture of one.

Baby steps should be the theme of your adventure. You and your family members should venture to the limits of your comfort zone, but not any further. The tone you want to set is a good-natured, mutually supportive approach to the things that make you nervous.

THAT REMINDS ME

Do a quick online search of the most common fears and phobias. Read the list aloud and see how many of your family's fears are represented. Talk about whether there's any comfort in knowing that countless other people struggle with the same fears that you do.

Be transparent with your family members as you talk about ways in which your fears have impacted your life. If you've tried different methods for overcoming your phobias, share them and talk about which ones worked (even temporarily) and which ones didn't.

See if any of your family members can trace their fears or phobias to a certain event or whether they've just had them for as long as they can remember.

FAMILY DEVOTIONS

Say something like this: *The gospel of Matthew tells the story of a terrifying situation and a man who faced his fear in a dramatic way.* Have someone read Matthew 14:22–33. In the passage, Jesus' disciples are in a boat, at night, on a choppy sea, when they see something coming toward them—walking *on* the water's surface.

Ask, *How would you have reacted if you'd been in the boat that night and saw someone walking toward you in the midst of the storm?* If no one else mentions it, suggest that many people would jump to the conclusion that the disciples did: that they were seeing a ghost.

Say something like this: *Even after the disciples realized that it was Jesus walking on the water, they were still facing a frightening situation. A nighttime storm at sea in those days was a matter of life and death. So why did Peter jump out of the boat in*  *the midst of the squall?* If no one else mentions it, point out that Peter saw a chance to get closer to Jesus by facing his fears.

Ask, *Why did Peter start to sink?* If no one else mentions it, point out that he took his eyes off Jesus and started focusing on his fears again.

Pray together, thanking God for inviting us into His presence when we feel afraid. Ask Him to give you perspective when it comes to your fears so that you can see that His power is greater than any anxiety we experience.

LANGUAGE OF THE DAY

There's a good chance that you or your spouse share a fear or phobia with one of your children. (If not, you may be able to empathize with one of your child's fears or phobias.) That lays the groundwork for some serious bonding time—something that will be especially meaningful to someone whose primary love language is Quality Time. Commiserate with son or daughter about how fear has affected—and still affects—you.

TO NEXT ADVENTURE

A VISIT TO THE MINORS

40

Support your local minor league team with a trip to the ballpark for a game.

GETTING READY

If you don't usually follow minor league baseball, do a little research before the game. Find information about the players on the team—who's having a good year, who got sent down from the major leagues, who's just coming back from an injury. See if you can find any human-interest angles as well—who came from an impoverished background, who volunteers in the community, who was never projected to make it in baseball. The more your family members know about the players, the more invested they may be in rooting for them.

You may also want to make sure that your family understands the minor-league system—how

Single A, Double A, and Triple A teams give players a chance to work on their skills and impress major league teams. Find out which major league team your minor league team is affiliated with. Talk about the well-known major leaguers who once played for the team you're going to see.

ADVENTURE TIME

"Come early and stay late" is the unspoken motto of most minor league teams, who often go to great lengths to ensure a memorable fan experience. If you arrive early, you may be able to take pictures with and get autographs from players and coaches. Many minor-league parks have skills challenges, where you can test the velocity and accuracy of your fastball, among other things. They also offer a variety of free games and activities for kids.

Whether your family members are baseball fans or not, encourage them to get into the spirit of the game. Join in the crowd chants. See if you can start one of your own. If you have restless kids, make a plan for what you will do at the end of each inning so that they always have something to look forward to. For example, you might hit the hot dog stand, walk around the stadium, hunt down a cotton candy vendor, take some goofy photos to post on social media, visit the nacho concession—you get the idea.

Some stadiums feature a family picnic area beyond the outfield fences. You could save money by packing your own meal. If you stick around after the game, you may be able to catch a fireworks show or let your kids run the bases.

THAT REMINDS ME

If there's a lull in the game, talk about what life must be like for a professional baseball player.

Point out that game day represents only a small percentage of a player's responsibilities. There's also traveling, practice, physical therapy, dealing with the media, making appearances in the community, eating right, and working out.

Take a poll to see how many of your family members think they would enjoy being a professional athlete—and, if so, in what sport. Talk about which aspects of the job would come easily to them and which would seem like hard work.

FAMILY DEVOTIONS

Say something like this: *Baseball players aren't the only people who have crowds watching them.* Have someone read Hebrews 12:1 ("Therefore, since we are surrounded by such a great cloud of witnesses, let us throw off everything that hinders and the sin that so easily entangles. And let us run with perseverance the race marked out for us"). Explain that the cloud of witnesses includes those who have gone before us in the Christian faith.

Ask, *How does it make you feel to know that other believers have gone before you and want you to run the race well?* If anyone has a negative reaction, point out that, like the fans in the baseball stadium, our witnesses are cheering for us. They want to see us succeed.

Pray together, thanking God that He has surrounded us with support and encouragement, whether we can see it or not. Ask Him to help you and your family keep your cloud of witnesses in mind when you face temptations or difficult decisions.

LANGUAGE OF THE DAY

If Physical Touch is the primary love language of someone in your family, sit next to that person at the game. Work up a set of handshakes and high fives to use when certain events happen during the game. For example, you might use one handshake every time your pitcher strikes out an opponent. You might use another every time one of your players makes a great catch. You might do a high five with a twist whenever one of your players gets a hit. And you might do something *really* complex for a home run.

TO NEXT ADVENTURE

SPEED-GAMING:
VIDEO GAME STYLE

41

How many different video games can your family play in a single day?

GETTING READY

Your goal is to play as many different video games as possible. If you don't have a large video game collection, you may need to supplement it with some games borrowed from the library or from friends. You may also want to borrow a gaming system or two so that you can play a greater variety of games. Look for games that your whole family can enjoy together.

If you have someone in your family who's a complete novice when it comes to video games, you might want to give him or her a chance to get acquainted with some of the games before your Speed Gaming adventure begins.

ADVENTURE TIME

Your goal is to play as many different video games as possible *as a family*. That means you want to avoid games that may become too immersive for a single player. Keep the pace quick. After one game of Wii bowling or one race on Mario Kart, move on to the next game. If you discover some favorites along the way, go back and play them *after* you've gone through the rest of your collection.

If you want to make it a competition, write down the winner of each game and award a prize to the person who wins the most games overall.

THAT REMINDS ME

Talk a little about how video games have changed since you were young. Describe the games you used to play, how long you used to play them, and how your parents felt about it.

If you have a serious gamer (or gamers) in your family, talk about the usual parental concerns using an unusual, nonconfrontational approach. Say something like this: *Imagine that you have a friend named Chris. One day, Chris's parents pull you aside to talk about Chris's gaming habits. They come to you because you're Chris's most trustworthy friend. They say, "We're really worried about how much time Chris is spending gaming. It seems like he's lost interest in everything else."* What would you say to them? Encourage your gamer to share his or her real feelings, and not just what he or she thinks you want to hear.

If your child seems open to the discussion, ask a few more questions: *What would you say if Chris's parents were worried that he didn't seem to have many friends beyond his gaming circle?*

What if they were worried about his grades? What advice would you give them about dealing with a serious gamer? How would they know when something was really wrong?

FAMILY DEVOTIONS

Have your family members take turns reading Ecclesiastes 3:1–8. The passage emphasizes the importance of "seasons" in our life, understanding that there is a time for "every activity under the heavens." That means there's a time to plant and a time to uproot, a time to tear down and a time to build, a time to weep and a time to laugh, a time to mourn and time to dance, a time to be silent and a time to speak.

Ask, *What happens when one "season" extends beyond its natural time? For example, what if the time to laugh stretched on and on and on?* If no one else mentions it, suggest that other "seasons" would get shortened. The result would be an unbalanced life, one that isn't following its God-given flow.

Ask, *How can we keep balance in our life?* If no one else mentions it, suggest that keeping track of our time is a good start. It's easy to lose track of time when we're doing things we enjoy. But that takes away time from other important seasons of life: our social time, our work time, our spiritual time, our family time, our active time, our educational time. And that leads to imbalance.

Pray together, thanking God for the variety of seasons He created for us to enjoy. Ask Him to help you and your family understand the importance of experiencing different seasons and recognize when things start to get unbalanced.

LANGUAGE OF THE DAY

You can make this adventure memorable for a family member whose primary love language is Physical Touch. Before you start, announce that anyone who beats you in a game gets tickled. For good measure, add that anyone who gets beat *by* you in a game also gets tickled.

TO NEXT ADVENTURE

BACKWARD DAY

42

**In the mood for a silly diversion?
Try doing everything backward for a day.**

GETTING READY

Give your family a hint as to what kind of day is
coming by turning all of the pictures in your house
to the wall. Turn the couches and chairs in your
family room so that they're facing *away* from the
TV. Turn your dining room chairs so that they're
facing *away* from the table. In short, if something in
your house can be turned backward, turn it backward.

ADVENTURE TIME

The question you have to ask yourself is this: How
backward do you want your day to be? An easy
place to start would be to flip your meal order.
Serve dinner in the morning and breakfast in the

evening. And when you serve dinner, why not start with dessert and end with appetizers?

Read bedtime stories to your kids as soon as they wake up. Brush your teeth *before* you eat. Watch one of your favorite movies or TV episodes in rewind mode, from the end credits to the very beginning.

If you don't mind stares or questions from curious onlookers, take a backward walk around the block or through your neighborhood. How will you dress for the stroll? It would be easy to wear a hat backward, but what about your shirt or sweatshirt? How many clothes can you wear backward?

You could try to play a board game like Sorry, Candyland or Chutes and Ladders backward. Players start with their pieces in the finish position and try to work their way back to the start position.

If you want to add a degree of challenge to your adventure, you could announce that whenever you give a signal, everyone has to *talk* backward. They have to say the words of every sentence in reverse order until you give another signal.

THAT REMINDS ME

Brainstorm a list of other things a person might do backward and then rank them on a scale of 1 to 10, based on how difficult or dangerous each one would be. For example, driving a car backward in your driveway might be a 2; driving a car backward on a busy interstate would probably be a 10. Walking upstairs backward might be a 2; walking downstairs backward might be a 7.

Talk about things that seem "backward" in the world today. For example, professional athletes (who play a game for a living) make at least twenty times more than schoolteachers (who mold lives and inspire kids to reach their potential). Biblical Christianity is something that much of the world considers to be backwards today. As Christians, what are some ways in which the Bible calls us to live "backwards," at least according to society? In the reality of the kingdom of God, it is society that is backwards. Brainstorm some ideas for making things not so backward.

FAMILY DEVOTIONS

Say something like this: *No matter how many backward things we do today, we will never come close to being as backward as Jesus was in Mark 10:35–45. Keep in mind that in Jesus' day, people had the same ideas about greatness that people today have. They thought that greatness meant being powerful and having many people serve you. Even Jesus' disciples believed that. But look at what Jesus told them.*

Have your family members take turns reading the passage. Ask, *According to Jesus, if you want to be great in the way God measures greatness, what do you have to do?* If no one else mentions it, point out that the more willing you are to serve others, the greater you are in God's eyes. No one is greater than Jesus because no one is more of a servant than He was.

Ask, *What does it mean to serve others?* If no one else mentions it, point out that serving others means putting other people's needs ahead of ours, being willing to sacrifice our time and energy for someone else. It means having a humble spirit. It means being joyful, and not jealous, when good things happen to others.

LANGUAGE OF THE DAY

Rowers often use hats with mirrors attached to them so that they can see where they are going. These hats are available online, as are various mirror attachments that can be used in other sports, such as cycling. They would make a great souvenir of your Backward Day adventure—and an ideal expression of love for someone whose primary love language is Receiving Gifts.

TO NEXT ADVENTURE

I'M NOT MYSELF RIGHT NOW

43

For one hour, everyone in your house must pretend to be someone else.

GETTING READY

The only preparation you'll need to do for this adventure is to make sure that everyone understands the ground rules. You'll set a timer for one hour. During that hour, no one is allowed to act or speak like himself or herself. Everyone must take on the personality of someone else in your house.

You want to set the right tone for this adventure. Emphasize the importance of being respectful and sensitive in your portrayals. You don't want to hurt anyone's feelings. It's okay to playfully imitate one another, as long as there's no mean-spiritedness in it.

If you want to make the adventure a little more challenging, announce that every fifteen minutes everyone has to take on a *new* personality.

ADVENTURE TIME

Encourage your family members to focus on harmless quirks of the people they're imitating. For example, maybe someone in your family likes to arrange the food on his plate in a very specific way. Or perhaps someone likes to hum while she brushes her teeth. Or perhaps someone has some highly unusual dance moves—in which case, you should probably get some video of the imitator and imitatee in a dance-off.

If everyone agrees to it, allow your family members to wear clothing items of the person they're imitating. (Snap a few photos of your family members dressed in each other's clothes—not necessarily for public consumption, but for a prime place in your family photo album.)

Remind your family members periodically that this adventure is a celebration of one another's uniqueness.

 ## THAT REMINDS ME

Talk about the difference between having fun with someone, as you did with these imitations, and being the butt of jokes. Share some examples from your own life of when you were the butt of a joke or the object of teasing. Talk about how it felt. Encourage your family members to share their own stories.

Spend some time talking about why people try to make others feel bad. Talk about how you can avoid hurting others with your teasing and jokes. Then talk about what God wants us to do when other people are hurting us.

Say something like this: *I hope no one was offended or hurt by our adventure. All of our imitations were done in a spirit of fun.*

FAMILY DEVOTIONS

Say something like this: *There's an old saying that goes, "Imitation is the sincerest form of flattery." That means it's really an honor to be imitated. The reason we're able to imitate one another is that we*

know each other so well. We pay attention to one another. And that makes God happy.

Have someone read Romans 12:10 ("Be devoted to one another in love. Honor one another above yourselves"). Point out that the apostle Paul seems to be challenging us to see how much honor we can bring to one another.

Ask, *How do you bring honor to someone?* If no one else mentions it, suggest that you find what is admirable in the person and call attention to it—not necessarily in public ways, but in private conversations.

Have someone read Philippians 2:3–4 ("Do nothing out of selfish ambition or vain conceit. Rather, in humility value others above yourselves, not looking to your own interests but each of you to the interests of the others"). Ask, *What happens in a family or church where everyone puts the interests of others first?* If no one else mentions it, point out that everyone gets their interests met.

Pray together, thanking God for your family and the closeness you share. Ask Him to give you the wisdom, patience, and endurance to strengthen and deepen your relationships as your kids grow older.

LANGUAGE OF THE DAY

If Receiving Gifts is the primary love language of one of your family members, this adventure offers a golden opportunity to demonstrate love in a profound way. With your imitation, you are saying, in effect, "I know what you're like because I've watched you closely for years." With a well-chosen gift, you are saying, "I know what you like because your happiness has been important to me for years." The gift you choose doesn't have to be expensive, as long as it reflects the person's interests.

TO NEXT ADVENTURE

DID IT IN A MINUTE

44   **Plan a series of challenges that must be completed in sixty seconds or less.**

GETTING READY

In order to know where to set the bar for each challenge—that is, how many repetitions your contestants must complete in a minute—you (and perhaps one of your young kids) will need to try it several times and keep track of your results. Your goal for each challenge is to set a bar that is achievable, yet challenging, for everyone in your family.

ADVENTURE TIME

Offer a relatively equal mix of physical, mental, and luck-based challenges so that you don't favor one family member's skills above another. Your possibilities are endless, but here a few ideas to get you started. (You will fill in the number for each challenge, based on your practice attempts.)

In one minute, contestants must . . .

- roll a 7 or 11 ___ times with a pair of dice

- jump a rope ___ times without a miss

- move a cookie from their forehead to their mouth without using their hands

- bounce on a pogo stick ___ times in a row before their foot touches the ground

- move ___ M&Ms from one plate to another using only the suction from a straw

- build a pyramid-shaped tower using ___ plastic Solo cups and then disassemble the tower and return the cups to a single stack

- make ___ three-pointers or free throws in a basketball hoop in a row

THAT REMINDS ME

Point out that this adventure involved a little pressure—a *fun* kind of pressure, but pressure still the same. Ask your family members to list other situations that involve pressure. If no one else mentions it, point out that many people feel pressure at school—pressure to fit in, pressure to look a certain way, pressure to get good grades. Invite the students in your family to add to that list.

Many people feel pressure at sports—pressure to win, pressure to live up to the expectations of parents and coaches, pressure to attend every practice even though you have a million others things to do. Invite the athletes in your family to add to that list.

Many people feel pressure at work—pressure to work late hours, pressure to sacrifice home life in order to advance, pressure to finish projects on time and under budget. Invite family members with jobs to add to that list.

Many parents feel pressure—pressure to juggle work life and home life, pressure to make wise decisions regarding their kids, pressure to maintain a spotless house and a family that looks good on social media. Invite your spouse to add to that list.

Many people feel pressure all the time—pressure to be something they're not, pressure to pretend like everything is okay when it's not, pressure that they can't even explain. Invite everyone to add to that list.

FAMILY DEVOTIONS

Have someone read Matthew 11:28–30 ("Come to me, all you who are weary and burdened, and I will give you rest. Take my yoke upon you and learn from me, for I am gentle and humble in heart, and you will find rest for your souls. For my yoke is easy and my burden is light"). Ask, *How can we find the peace and rest that Jesus promises when we are feeling pressured?* If no one else mentions it, suggest that the key is daily prayer. As soon as you start to feel pressure, you give it to the Lord in prayer and ask for His strength, guidance, and wisdom in dealing with it.

Ask, *In addition to praying, what else can we do when we face pressurized situations?* If no one else mentions it, suggest that you can share your burdens with one another—and with others who love and want the best for you.

Pray together, praising the Lord for His limitless strength. Thank Him for caring about you and your family enough to carry your burdens and relieve the pressure you feel. Ask Him to give you the strength to work through the pressurized situations you face and the wisdom to know when to turn them over to Him.

LANGUAGE OF THE DAY

If Physical Touch is the primary love language of someone in your family, make sure you include challenges that require pairs to work in physical contact with one another. For example, if your kids are small, you might do a challenge in which you have to run two laps around your house, with them standing on your shoes, in sixty seconds.

TO NEXT ADVENTURE

SPEED-GAMING: SPORTS STYLE

45

**See how many different outdoor sports
your family can play in a single day.**

GETTING READY

You can make this sports-filled day run smoothly
with a little advance work. The most important
thing you'll need to do is scout locations in your
area. Where is the nearest public baseball diamond,
football field, outdoor basketball court, tennis
court, sand volleyball pit, track (with a jumping
pit), par-3 golf course, miniature golf course, and
other outdoor sports venues? Once you have an idea
of what you have to work with, you can begin to
plan your adventure.

ADVENTURE TIME

Set an agenda for your day, based on the sports you
choose. If, for example, you want to play golf (par 3),

you may need to get a tee time and work around that. At each site, quickly outline the game you're going to play and the rules you're going to follow. If there are people in your family who are considerably better at a particular sport than everyone else, create some "equalizers" to make games competitive. For example, if you have a varsity basketball player in your family, you may decide that she has to dribble and shoot with her off hand.

Your goal with this adventure is not so much hard-fought competitiveness as it is quick-paced fun. Play a short game of basketball (or perhaps Horse or Pig) and then move on to football, volleyball, or something else. If you keep moving on to the next sport, no one will have time to stew over losses. If you play as teams, make sure you switch them up after each sport so that everyone gets a chance to play with everyone else. Tweak the game play of each sport, as necessary, to give everyone a chance to shine.

THAT REMINDS ME

As you begin each new sport, talk about the specific skills that are necessary for that sport. For example, baseball requires excellent hand-eye coordination, quick reflexes, a strong throwing arm, and speed. Football requires strength, power, speed, and hand-eye coordination. Golf also requires hand-eye coordination, along with lower-body strength and the ability to concentrate. Talk about which sport each of your family members seems best suited for, based on natural abilities,

Point out that the fact that there are people who excel at each of the different sports is a testament to God's incredible design of our bodies.

FAMILY DEVOTION

Have someone read Romans 12:1 ("Therefore, I urge you, brothers and sisters, in view of God's mercy, to offer your bodies as a living sacrifice, holy and pleasing to God—this is your true and proper worship"). Explain that a sacrifice is something we give to God. Ask, *How do we give our bodies to God while we're still using them?* If no one else mentions it, suggest that we do it by acknowledging that our bodies don't belong to us, but to God; He created them so that we might use them to bring glory to Him. We sacrifice our bodies by making ourselves available to be used by God.

Ask, *How can we take care of our bodies in a way that pleases God?* If no one else mentions it, suggest that we do it by refusing to do things that are harmful to our bodies. We do it by exercising, eating right, and getting the sleep we need. We do it by training our bodies to be the best they can be. We do it by exercising our minds, too. We do it by making the most of what God has given us and then giving Him the glory for it.

LANGUAGE OF THE DAY

If Physical Touch is the primary love language of one of your family members, announce one final sport in which the two of you will compete: wrestling. Challenge him or her to a playful wrestling match—one that features plenty of bear hugs, overhead lifts, and rolling around.

TO NEXT ADVENTURE

LOCKED OUT

Close the door to your house and spend a day outside.

46

GETTING READY

In order to make this adventure as outdoorsy as possible, you'll need to prepare thoroughly. Try to anticipate everything your family will need for the day: food and drinks (stored in a cooler), insect repellant, sunscreen, towels, a change of clothes—plus anything else you can think of. Remember, once the adventure begins, your goal is to not go inside for anything (except restroom visits).

You'll also need to keep an eye on the forecast. The more pleasant your weather is, the more pleasant your adventure will be.

ADVENTURE TIME

The ages of your kids will factor into how strictly you observe the "rules" of this adventure. If you think your family would enjoy the challenge of outdoor living for an entire day, announce that the only time someone is allowed in the house is to use the restroom—or for a medical emergency. Aside from that, the only time anyone will not be outside is when you're in the car, heading to an outdoor destination.

What you choose to do outside will depend on your family's interests and the options available to you in your area. Your first stop might be a botanical garden or a zoo. (You'll just have to make it a point to avoid indoor exhibits.) Your next stop might be a water park. Once your family is exhausted from running, splashing, swimming, and sliding, head to a local park. There, you can string up some hammocks, relax, and enjoy a picnic dinner. Cap off your day with a drive-in movie. Set up lawn chairs and enjoy the film al fresco.

If you want to take this idea to its logical conclusion, pitch a tent in your backyard and sleep outside, making it a twenty-four-hour adventure.

 ## THAT REMINDS ME

Since your theme is outdoors, keep a conversation running throughout the day about what you would do if your family were suddenly shipwrecked and stranded on a desert island.

Start from the beginning of your imaginary scenario. How big is the island? What kind of natural features does it have? Are there dangerous animals or insects living on it? What supplies and debris from the ship washed up on shore with you? Once you have the "lay of the land," you can start brainstorming your survival ideas.

Draw on any scouting or camping experience (or years of watching *Survivor*) to decide what you should and shouldn't do. What factors would you need to consider before building a shelter? What materials would you use? How would you start a fire and keep it going? How would you protect yourselves from the elements? Where would you get food to eat and water to drink?

Keep coming back to this scenario throughout the day, imagining your progress on the island. Talk about whether you would try to signal ships or planes or build a raft and try to reach mainland.

FAMILY DEVOTIONS

Say something like this: *All of this outdoor living makes me think of a Bible story from the Old Testament. David was a faithful servant of King Saul. But Saul hated David because he was jealous of him. In fact, he tried to kill David. So David and the men who were loyal to him fled. And King Saul and his army chased them.*

Have your family members take turns reading 1 Samuel 23:14–15, 24–25; 24:3. The verses describe the places David and his men had to live while they were on the run from Saul. They camped in the wilderness, on hills, in several deserts, and even in a cave. Ask, *What do you think was the worst part about how David and his men were living?* If no one else mentions it, suggest that being vulnerable to the elements 24/7 was likely a difficult adjustment.

Ask, *What do you think was the best part?* If no one else mentions it, point out that God took care of David and his men. He protected them. Talk about whether it's possible that being out in nature made David feel closer to God.

Explain that David stayed faithful to God. He had opportunities to kill Saul, but would not do it. When Saul finally died, David replaced him as king.

LANGUAGE OF THE DAY

You can make this adventure especially memorable for a family member whose primary love language is Physical Touch. Strap a hammock to two trees in your yard and spend some time lying in it with them. Talk, if you want to; otherwise, just enjoy spending time side by side.

TO NEXT ADVENTURE

PENNIES GALORE

Plan a day around that humblest of coins, the penny.

47

GETTING READY

The best way to prepare for this adventure is to cash in a few dollar bills so that you have a surplus of pennies on hand. You may also want to purchase some coin books, in case your kids decide they want to start collecting pennies.

ADVENTURE TIME

With a little creativity, you can incorporate penny-related activities into every part of your day. Here are a few ideas to get you started.

Build a series of choices into your day that must be decided with the flip of a coin (a penny, to be more precise). Let your family members take turns flipping a coin. For example, when your family wakes up, tell them that you're going to make either pancakes (heads) or scrambled eggs (tails) for breakfast.

Hold a treasure hunt in your house to find as many pennies as you can in fifteen minutes. Offer some kind of reward if your family members can find, say, five pennies scattered throughout your house and car. (Pennies that are in piggy banks or coin jars don't count.)

Challenge your family members to see how many pennies they can stack on their elbow and catch in their hand in one quick movement.

Give your kids coin books (the kind coin collectors use) and dump a big pile of pennies in the middle of your dining room table. Sort through the pennies to see if you can find any to add to the coin books.

Take some pennies to a nearby fountain and let your kids throw them in and make some wishes.

THAT REMINDS ME

Throughout the day, give your family members "a penny for their thoughts." Explain that when you hand them the coin, they have to tell you what they're thinking about at that moment. This may open up some interesting lines of conversation. Build some time into your adventure to enjoy such converstions.

Talk about how many pennies it would take to buy certain things. For example, in order to buy a $35,000 car, you would need 3.5 *million* pennies. In order to buy a $250,000 house, you would need 25 *billion* pennies. While those may seem like impossible numbers, explain that there have been collectors who cashed in more than one million pennies at one time. Challenge your family members to see how many pennies they can collect in the next month.

FAMILY DEVOTIONS

Say something like this: *A penny may not seem like much, but there's a story in the Bible in which small coins meant a lot to Jesus.* Have someone read Luke 21:1–4. In the passage, Jesus watches rich people place their large offerings in the temple treasury. But when He sees a widow place two small copper coins in the treasury, He is truly moved.

Say something like this: *A copper coin was the penny of Jesus' day. The rich people were giving big bucks to the treasury. Why did Jesus say the widow had put in more than they did?* If no one else mentions it, point out that the rich people gave a lot because they had a lot. The widow gave two copper coins because that was all she had.

Ask, *Why did the widow give God everything she had to live on?* If no one else mentions it, suggest that she understood where the coins had come from. God gave to her, so she gave back to Him. She also knew what God could do with two small copper coins. She trusted God to take care of her.

Pray together, thanking God for what He has given your family. Ask Him to help you and your family members maintain the spirit of the widow when it comes to giving.

LANGUAGE OF THE DAY

If Receiving Gifts is the primary love language of one of your family members, start his or her penny collection with a relatively valuable or desirable coin. You can find what you're looking for by visiting a coin shop or an online store.

TO NEXT ADVENTURE

Celebrate all things water-related with your family.

48

GETTING READY

If you want to save time (and avoid headaches) for your actual adventure, fill your water balloons in advance. In the heat of battle, they tend to get used up quickly, so make sure you create an arsenal worthy of your adventure. Fill a wading pool (or two) with engorged balloons of various sizes. Declare them off-limits until the water-balloon fight officially begins.

You may also want to make sure that your family members are on-board for cleaning up after the water balloon fight.

ADVENTURE TIME

The centerpiece of your water adventure should be a visit to a waterpark or your local pool. Instead of going your separate ways once you get there, however, stick together as a family. Make up games, contests, and challenges to do together. If one person wants to go down a slide, everyone should follow.

Supplement your time at the waterpark or pool with as many other water-related activities as you squeeze into a single day. Choose teams for a water-balloon fight and then let it devolve into a free-for-all, like all water-balloon fights do.

Give everyone water guns at the beginning of the day and announce that all family members are fair game to be squirted for the entire day, as long as they're outdoors.

Add any other water-related ideas that you think would appeal to your family.

THAT REMINDS ME

Talk about the importance and power of water. Explain that 71% of the earth—and about 60% of our bodies—is made up of water. Water keeps us alive. A person can go more than twenty-one days without food, but can go only three or four days without water.

Water has the power to enrich or destroy large areas. Just the right amount of water can make land fertile and able to produce food. Too little water causes drought, which can kill and uproot entire cultures. Too much water causes floods, which can destroy and kill in an instant.

Point out that people have built dams and canals to try to harness the power of water, but only the Lord can control it.

Genesis 1 describes how God separated the waters above from the waters below during creation. Genesis 6–9 describes how He used water to bring judgment on the earth during the flood. Exodus 14 describes how He parted the waters of the Red Sea so that the Israelites could walk through it on dry land. In Exodus 17, He brings water from a rock in the wilderness. In Matthew 14, Jesus walks on the surface of the sea. And in Mark 4, He calms a raging storm at sea with just a few words.

FAMILY DEVOTIONS

Say something like this: *That's not all the Bible says about water.* Have someone read John 7:37–39. In the passage, Jesus invites anyone who is thirsty to come to Him and drink. Ask, *What are people thirsty for when they come to Jesus?* If no one else mentions it, suggest that some people are thirsty for eternal life, some people for forgiveness, some people for hope, and some people for meaning, among other things.

Point out that the passage makes it clear what the flowing "rivers of living water" is. Jesus is talking about the Holy Spirit, who fills people's hearts when they give their lives to Him.

Ask, *What happens when the living water flows through us?* If no one else mentions it, suggest that the Holy Spirit quenches our spiritual thirst by helping us in every area of our walk with Christ. He makes our Bible study more meaningful and our prayers more powerful. You might also suggest that

the Holy Spirit's work in *our* lives can quench other people's spiritual thirst. They see the difference He makes inside us and become curious about what He can do for them.

Pray together, thanking God for the gift of His Holy Spirit. Ask Him to continue working in the lives of your family members to strengthen and deepen your relationship with Christ.

LANGUAGE OF THE DAY

If Physical Touch is the primary love language of one of your family members, make sure you engage in some "chicken fights" at the pool. Put them on your shoulders and do battle with another pair of family members. The pair that knocks the other one down wins the fight.

TO NEXT ADVENTURE

A GLIMPSE OF THE FUTURE

What do you and your family members hope to be doing twenty years from now? Here's an adventure that will allow you to preview your plans together.

49

GETTING READY

Before the adventure, schedule a brief family time during which each person gets to talk about their plans for the future. Encourage your kids to share their thoughts about what career they might like to pursue or where they might like to live one day. You and your spouse can talk about potential career changes or retirement plans.

Once you have an idea of what each person's tentative future plans are, make some arrangements to explore the various plans. For example, if your child's dream is to become a firefighter, arrange a visit to a local fire station. Give your child an opportunity to talk to real-life firefighters and find out what they do. If your spouse's post-retirement dream is to travel the country, plan a visit to an RV showroom.

ADVENTURE TIME

Your adventure will depend on what you and your family members identify as your future plans. In addition to the previously mentioned visits to a fire station and RV showroom, you might talk to a local doctor or visit a school classroom after hours to find out from a teacher what his or her job entails. If your spouse's post-retirement plan is to spend time in the yard, you may visit a garden or landscaping store. If it's someone's goal to live in a certain area of the world, you might watch a travelogue about the region. Whatever you do, make sure your day is fun and informative.

THAT REMINDS ME

Spend some time talking about what you wanted to be when you were a kid—or what you thought the future held for you. Chances are, you entertained several different possibilities. Share the most fanciful one first—a secret dream or plan that may come as a surprise to your family members. Encourage your spouse to do the same. If your kids are old enough, ask them to share some of their old dreams and plans for the future.

FAMILY DEVOTIONS

Say something like this: *We may not know exactly what the future holds, but we know who holds the future. God's Word gives us comfort and encouragement about what God has planned for us.*

Have someone read Jeremiah 29:11 ("'For I know the plans I have for you,' declares the LORD, 'plans to prosper you and not to harm you, plans to give you hope and a future'"). Ask, *How does it make you feel to know that God has thoughts about* your

future? If no one else mentions it, point out that, for some people, it might be comforting to realize that God has a future in mind for them. After all, His plans are perfect. For others, though, it may cause anxiety. They may be afraid that God's plans don't coincide with theirs. Or they may become stressed at the thought of having to figure out what God's plans are.

Have someone read Proverbs 16:3 ("Commit to the LORD whatever you do, and he will establish your plans"). Ask, *How can we commit our works to the Lord?* If no one else mentions it, suggest that we can use the gifts and abilities that He has given us. We can pray about the decisions we make and ask God to guide us through the promptings of His Holy Spirit. We can make sure that we give Him the glory and praise for our successes. When we're certain that we're doing God's will, we can persevere through hard times and refuse to let setbacks and occasional failures deter us.

Pray together, thanking God for equipping you for the future that awaits you—even if you don't know what that future is. Ask Him to give your family a sense of peace, comfort, and excitement about what lies ahead for each of you.

LANGUAGE OF THE DAY

You can make this adventure special for a family member whose primary love language is Words of Affirmation. Take some time, as a family, to affirm one another's future plans. Talk about the specific qualities you see in each person—their God-given gifts and abilities—that will help him or her succeed in his or her chosen path.

TO NEXT ADVENTURE

REMEMBER

Play some memory games as you celebrate cherished family memories together.

50

GETTING READY

Set the tone for your adventure by playing some of your favorite family videos. If you have (a) time and (b) video-editing software and skills, put together a compilation of your favorite moments from each person in your family. If you can put a date and context to each clip, it would be even better. Encourage your family members to share their own recollections of each event.

ADVENTURE TIME

The board game Memory would be ideal for this adventure. Players take turns turning over cards, trying to find a match. If they find a match, they keep the cards. If not, they turn the cards back over. The key to the game is remembering where various cards are. If you don't have the game, you can use playing cards instead. Players must find matching numbers or face cards. Another variation is to use duplicate family photos to play the game.

Another option is to place a variety of items on a table and cover them with a tablecloth. The items may include anything from a fork to a shoehorn to a few coins to a book on herbal gardening. It might be fun to use some family keepsakes or family photos for this activity. It doesn't matter what you use, as long as it's an unusual assortment. The way the game works is this. You will lift the tablecloth for 15 seconds, and players will try to memorize the items that are on the table. Replace the tablecloth and let players take turns trying to list the things they saw on the table. The player who can recall the most is the winner.

THAT REMINDS ME

While you play your games, share some of your favorite family memories. One way to do this is to name a place, time, or event and have family members shout out their favorite memory about it. For example, you might say, "The cabin in Tennessee" or "Grandma's old house in the country" or "Last Thanksgiving," prompting your family to share their favorite memories of each one.

If you have a loved one who struggles with Alzheimer's or dementia, this may be a good time to help your younger family members understand why the disease is so devastating to your family. Explain that memories are one of the things that bind us together. When someone starts to lose those memories, it can feel like our connection is unraveling. Not being recognized by someone who's loved you your entire life is a devastating thing. That's why we have to hold on tight to our own memories of that person.

FAMILY DEVOTIONS

Ask, *Besides past family events, what are some important things to remember?* If no one else mentions it, point out that it's important to remember how to do the things we do every day, such as ride a bike or use a microwave. It's also important to remember the things we learn at school and at work, since we will need to apply them later. Most important of all, though, it's important to remember God's Word.

Have someone read Deuteronomy 11:18–20. ("Fix these words of mine in your hearts and minds; tie them as symbols on your hands and bind them on your foreheads. Teach them to your children, talking about them when you sit at home and when you walk along the road, when you lie down and when you get up. Write them on the doorframes of your houses and on your gates"). Explain that in Old Testament times, some Jewish people wore phylacteries, which were small boxes that contained scrolls of Scripture, on their forehead and arm. They literally kept God's Word with them at all times.

Ask, *What is the best way for us to keep God's Word fresh in our memories?* If no one else mentions it, suggest memorizing key verses—ones that can offer comfort, encouragement, and strength when we need them most. Another way is simply to spend time in God's Word—lots and lots of time. The more familiar you become with something, the more memories you create. Point out, too, that parents play a role in helping their kids keep God's Word fresh in their memories. They do it by talking about God's Word frequently at home and applying it to daily life.

LANGUAGE OF THE DAY

There are journals available that contain writing prompts—questions and sentence starters that encourage you to share specific memories. Buy one and fill it out. Put your thoughts and recollections into writing. Give it to a family member whose primary love language is Receiving Gifts. It may or may not mean much at the moment, but someday it may become an invaluable treasure to them.

TO NEXT ADVENTURE

TRAVELING ABROAD IN THE COMFORT OF YOUR HOME

Transform your home into a house from a foreign country.

51

GETTING READY

After you choose a country, spend some time researching it as a family. If your kids are old enough, you might assign them specific areas to research about the country: food, language, culture, and pastimes. Give everyone a chance to present their findings at a family meeting. Using a white board or a large piece of paper, write down bits of information you can use for transforming your house.

ADVENTURE TIME

You may choose a country your family has visited, a place your ancestors came from, or a place that seems exotic and interesting to you. Post pictures of the country and its people throughout your house. Help your kids find it on a globe or in an atlas.

If there is an international grocery store in your area, visit it as a family. See if you can find food and products from the country you chose. If not, search online for recipes from the country and try your hand at making them.

Search also for music from the country and, if possible, create a playlist that you can use as a soundtrack for your adventure. Look for family-friendly movies that were made in your chosen country—or movies that deal with that country.

See if you can find some language-learning software from the library and spend some time as a family learning to say a few words and phrases in the language of your country. If your family enjoys craft projects, have them create and color the flag of your nation.

Supplement these ideas with some of your own as you celebrate a foreign culture.

THAT REMINDS ME

Share what you know about what life is like for the people in your country. Is the majority of the population wealthy or impoverished? Do many struggle to survive? If so, what are the causes of the struggle? Is the nation war-torn? If so, what is the root of the conflict? Has it recently suffered a natural disaster?

What is the dominant religion in the country? What role does Christianity play in people's lives? The more you find out about the country, the more focused your discussion will be.

After you've given an overview, ask your family members to put themselves in the place of people who live in that country. Talk about the most pressing needs you would face, whether it's food and water, peace and safety, or knowledge of Jesus and God's Word.

After you've identified those needs, brainstorm some ideas as to how your family might help meet them.

FAMILY DEVOTIONS

Have someone read Matthew 28:18–20 ("Then Jesus came to them and said, 'All authority in heaven and on earth has been given to me. Therefore go and make disciples of all nations, baptizing them in the name of the Father and of the Son and of the Holy Spirit, and teaching them to obey everything I have commanded you. And surely I am with you always, to the very end of the age'"). Explain that God's plan was for Jesus' followers to continue His ministry—to tell people who didn't know Jesus all about Him. The disciples and other missionaries did that by traveling to distant countries and preaching there.

Ask, *How can we obey Jesus' command to make disciples of all nations?* If no one else mentions it, suggest that you and your family can pray regularly for the people of your country. You can get involved with Christian organizations that minister to the country. You can make connections through social media (if it's a developed country). It is likely there are immigrants from that country here in the United States. Perhaps you can get to know someone in your local community who is from that country and can pray for them personally.

Spend some time praying for the people in your chosen country. Lift up their specific needs to the Lord and ask Him to work His will in them. Pray that God will make Himself known to the people there.

LANGUAGE OF THE DAY

This adventure presents a golden opportunity to do something memorable for a family member whose primary love language is Receiving Gifts. Search online for a souvenir from your chosen country—perhaps a sign with the person's name written in the native language. Present the souvenir to him or her as a reminder of your adventure.

TO NEXT ADVENTURE

ON THIS DAY

Create a time capsule to be opened in ten years.

52

GETTING READY

Bring home a copy of your local newspaper and a copy of a national newspaper. Talk to your kids about things that are going on in your town and things that are going on in the country and world. You don't need to go into a lot of detail. Just help them understand the basics of the biggest news stories of the day. Your goal is to give them things to react to and report on as they create their contributions to the time capsule.

ADVENTURE TIME

The time capsule you create will be a "snapshot" of your family on that particular day. Put the two newspapers in the capsule to give it context, so that when you open it a decade later, you'll know what was going on locally and nationally on that day.

Ask each person in your family to write a letter or diary entry to put into the time capsule. Emphasize that no one will read it until the capsule is opened in ten years. Encourage your family members to talk about the state of their lives *at that moment.* How are they feeling and why? What are their biggest worries? What are they looking forward to? Who are their best friends? Who are their favorite teachers? What are their favorite and least favorite subjects in school? What are their favorite TV shows, movies, and songs? What was their last post on social media? What new technology are they obsessed with?

In the second part of their entry, encourage them to project their thoughts ten years into the future and talk about what they think their life will be like. Will they be in school? Will

they be working? If so, where? What kind of car will they be driving? What will the world be like? What will be their biggest worries?

Help your family members understand that the more effort they put into their entries, the more meaningful they will be when you open the time capsule. Your goal is to capture a day in the life of your family *now* so that you can compare it with life ten years from now.

Have your family members seal their entries in envelopes and place them in the time capsule. Seal the time capsule and put it in a place where you will forget about it for a long time.

THAT REMINDS ME

After the time capsule has been put away, spend some time imagining what your family will be like when you open the capsule ten years from now. Will you live in the same house? Will your kids be in college? Will they be married?

Encourage your family members to talk about their feelings about the future. Do they feel optimistic and eager to see what's going to happen? Or are they nervous about it?

FAMILY DEVOTIONS

Say to your children, *The next time we open this time capsule, you will be different people. Not only will you look different, you'll also think differently—just as God created you to do.*

Have someone read 1 Corinthians 13:11 ("When I was a child, I talked like a child, I thought like a child, I reasoned like a child. When I became a man, I put the ways of childhood behind me"). Ask, *What's the difference between the way a child sees the world and the way an adult sees the world?* If no one else mentions it, suggest that a child may be scared by things that an adult doesn't find scary at all.

Ask, *What are some things that change as you become an adult that allow you to see things differently?* If no one else mentions it, talk about experience. For example, after you've worried time and time again about things that turned out to be okay, you get some perspective. You get a better idea not only of how the world works, but of how *God* works.

LANGUAGE OF THE DAY

If Acts of Service is the primary love language of one of your family members, go out of your way to make this adventure as easy as possible for him or her. Create a page with writing prompts to help get the information you need without it feeling like an essay test. The prompts might include things like "My best friend is . . ." and "If I could do anything this weekend, it would be . . ."

INDEX OF FAMILY ADVENTURES
TIME COMMITMENT

One-Hour:
Thank-You Cards
All Things Nerf
Hide-and-Seek
Interviews
Something Old
Pillow Fight
How Many Can You Fit?
That's Not How the Story Ends
Mirror Games
Photobombing
Makeovers
Fun with Blindfolds
I'm Not Myself Right Now
Did It in a Minute
Remember
On This Day

Half-Day:
Bowling with a Twist
Library Scavenger Hunt
Bike Wash & Tune-Up Center
Create a Family Lip-Sync Video
Camera Art
Show Me How to Do That
A Grand Welcome
Adopt a Grandparent
Family vs. Family
Toilet Paper Olympics
Invention Exchange

Obstacle Course
Something New
Early Christmas Shopping
Indoor Camping
Book Challenge
A Visit to the Minors
Speed Gaming

All-Day:
Something Blue
Stealth Service
Foster a Pet
Volunteer Day
Cities to Explore
Switch Rooms
Every Day Is a Holiday
Something Borrowed
Make Up Your Own Holiday
Face Your Fears
Speed-Gaming: Video Game Style
Backward Day
Speed-Gaming: Sports Style
Locked Out
Pennies Galore
H2O
A Glimpse of the Future
Traveling Abroad in the Comfort
   of Your Home

LOVE LANGUAGE FOCUS

Acts of Service:
Library Scavenger Hunt
Foster a Pet
Bike Wash & Tune-Up Center
Switch Rooms
Every Day Is a Holiday
Invention Exchange
Indoor Camping
On This Day

Physical Touch:
Pillow Fight
How Many Can You Fit?
Family vs. Family
Book Challenge
A Visit to the Minors
Speed-Gaming: Video Game Style
Did It in a Minute
Speed-Gaming: Sports Style
Locked Out
H2O

Quality Time:
Something Old
Speed Gaming
Create a Family Lip-Sync Video
Mirror Games
Toilet Paper Olympics
Obstacle Course
Make Up Your Own Holiday
Fun with Blindfolds
Face Your Fears
Backward Day

Receiving Gifts:
All Things Nerf
Volunteer Day
That's Not How the Story Ends
Cities to Explore
Camera Art
Photobombing
A Grand Welcome
Something New
Early Christmas Shopping
I'm Not Myself Right Now
Pennies Galore
Remember
Traveling Abroad in the
   Comfort of Your Home

Words of Affirmation:
Thank-You Cards
Hide-and-Seek
Bowling with a Twist
Interviews
Something Blue
Stealth Service
Show Me How to Do That
Adopt a Grandparent
Something Borrowed
Makeovers
A Glimpse of the Future

LOCALE

Indoors:

Outdoors:

COST

Free:

Low Cost:

Thank-You Cards
Bike Wash & Tune-Up Center
Camera Art
Photobombing
Adopt a Grandparent
Family vs. Family
Toilet Paper Olympics
Every Day Is a Holiday
Makeovers
Locked Out
Pennies Galore
A Glimpse of the Future
Traveling Abroad in the Comfort
 of Your Home

Moderate Cost:

Bowling with a Twist
Something Blue
Foster a Pet
Cities to Explore
A Grand Welcome
Early Christmas Shopping
A Visit to the Minors
H2O

CAPTURE YOUR UNCOMMON FAMILY ADVENTURES!

Snap a photo of your fun family
adventures and share with
your friends on social media using

#52UncommonAdventures

FUN, CREATIVE, AND SPIRITUALLY ENGAGING — THESE ARE NO ORDINARY DATES

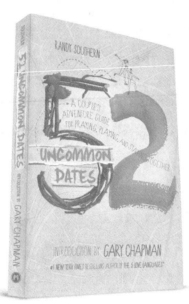

52 Uncommon Dates ignites a prayerful and playful connection between couples in a way that feels natural to schedule and relevant to real life. Fun, creative, and spiritually engaging, this powerful resource will spiritually energize your relationship, one date at a time.

978-0-8024-1174-7 | also available as an eBook

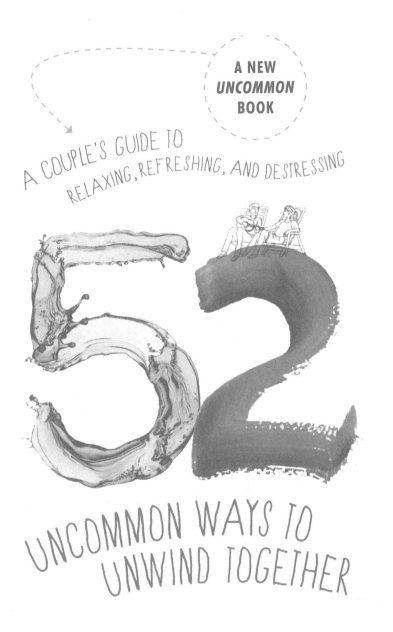

A NEW
UNCOMMON
BOOK

A COUPLE'S GUIDE TO
RELAXING, REFRESHING, AND DESTRESSING

52

UNCOMMON WAYS TO
UNWIND TOGETHER